The Amish are not a monolithic people. Some groups are harder to break free from than others. My own journey from the culture was difficult enough. At least I thought so, until I read Joe Keim's story.

Joe and Esther Keim emerged from a dark, harsh place, where hard choices had to be made about family, faith, and what was truly important to them. It was a tough road to travel, with a heavy price. Joe Keim recounts the faith and courage that carried them through in their darkest hours. But freedom for themselves was not enough; Joe and Esther Keim turned and reached out to others who were traveling the same path they had walked. Today, they minister to hundreds of young Amish people who are desperate to break free from their own dark, hard places.

This is a unique story of one man's astonishing journey from an Amish world unlike any I have ever known.

Ira Wagler
Author of *Growing Up Amish*

If you've ever been curious about the inner workings of Amish life, this book is for you. Joe captivates readers from the first word, keeping them glued to the page and wanting more. An honest, heart-wrenching true-life tale of one man's struggle to remain Amish. This is a must-read for anyone remotely interested in Amish life and customs.

J. Spredemann
Amish fiction author

Joe Keim's book mirrored much of my own experience of when I left the Amish church. I could truly feel his frustration with living under the absolute rule of the church and the fear of venturing out into the unknown *English* world. The devastation of losing all of your family and the only life you have ever known is something that is felt forever.

I commend his work with *Mission to Amish People*; I wish I would have had someone who was formerly Amish to help me transition into the modern world.

Misty Griffin
Author of *Tears of the Silenced*

Joe Keim has given us an honest, intriguing look into the world and choices of the Amish. His descriptions of life before and after are as plain-spoken and true as his presentation of scriptural grace and faith in Christ. I would have expected nothing less from Joe.

Dandi Daley Mackall
Author of *With Love, Wherever You Are*
www.dandibooks.com

S0-ACC-963

My People, The Amish, is Joe Keim's account of awakening to God's gift of grace. As a man born into a religion that often urges its members to work for grace from cradle to grave, Joe recounts how God led him full circle from leaving his Amish people, to ministering to his Amish people. Readers experience the passion born in Joe Keim the moment he took up Christ's cross and began his journey, his calling, and his service to many Amish and former Amish communities. I highly recommend Joe's book to anyone who wants to learn more about the Amish as well as for those who want to learn more about what a genuine relationship with God looks like.

Dee Yoder
Author of *The Miting: An Old Order Amish Novel*

This is a must for all to read! It's very transparent about how the Amish live and what they believe, and being formerly Amish, I can relate to a big part of the story. It can make you laugh in one chapter, and cry in the next one. Joe talks about his father and the relationship he has with him now. That spoke to me, and I pray for the same thing someday.

Samuel Girod
MAP Ministry missionary

When God took Joe Keim's hopeless, unsatisfied soul, and restored it with everlasting life in Christ Jesus, Joe became a new person. The hurt from his past didn't turn into bitterness; instead it fueled his passion to help others who, like him, wanted to leave the strict Amish religion. Religious traditions can sometimes tear a family apart, but Joe's prayer is that the love of our Lord and Savior would heal those broken families. I highly recommend this book to anyone seeking to know more about the Amish religion.

Naomi Mullet Stutzman
Author of *A Basketful of Broken Dishes*

My People, The Amish is a truly gripping story of Joe Keim and his life growing up Amish. It includes his journey, which would ultimately lead him to salvation in Jesus Christ, marriage to his childhood sweetheart, Esther, leaving the Amish way of life, and finding God's calling right where he didn't expect it. This is so much more than a story and history of the greatest minister to the Amish our country has known. I found myself in tears and the story personally challenged the depth of my walk with Jesus Christ. This was time well spent!

Stan Debro
Advisor for MAP Ministry

Written with a lot of soul. This read is a breath of fresh air.

Mose J. Gingerich

An exciting narrative of how God singled out a young Amish couple living in sin to do the miraculous. Joe has given us a simple textbook for understanding Amish culture and how to evangelize Amish people. There is no doubt of his love for God and his people. Thoroughly enjoyable.

Charlotte Wagner

This book is about a real-life illustration of biblical transformation through the gospel of Jesus Christ. Joe came to Bethel Baptist Church from the plain clothes lifestyle of the Amish to be discipled into a man of God. He is now leading one of the great ministries in North America, Mission to Amish People, reaching thousands for Christ. I have been his pastor for over thirty years and have watched the transformation of his life and ministry.

John A. Bouquet
Pastor, Bethel Baptist Church

Most Americans would think they understand what the Amish believe and how they live. In *My People, The Amish*, Joe Keim shares a story of brokenness, shunning, rejection, and beautiful redemption, telling it in a way that will affect your heart for the Amish, no matter your background or culture. This book also speaks truth clearly to those of any culture who are held hostage by a rules-based lifestyle, and reveals the love Joe and Esther Keim have for their Amish family. They live out that love through MAP, an organization of restoration and redemption for the glory of God.

Dolores M. Robinson
Portage Community Chapel, Ravenna, Ohio

Having been born and raised in the Amish religion, I share Joe's burden for "my people," who are still held captive in the Amish religion. I appreciate the honesty and transparency with which he shares his experiences of unbelievable spiritual confusion, turmoil, abuse, and anguish of the soul, which is indeed a reality for many in that religion. Joe is a shining trophy of God's grace; refusing to be embittered by his traumatic experiences, but rather exemplifying a heartfelt compassion for those still in spiritual darkness by reaching out to them. This book is a valuable resource for understanding the Amish mentality, and learning how to reach these people who need the gospel of Christ.

Mary Schrock
Author of *The Greater Inheritance*

Brethren, my heart's desire and prayer to God for Israel is, that they might be saved. For I bear them record that they have a zeal of God, but not according to knowledge. For they being ignorant of God's righteousness, and going about to establish their own righteousness, have not submitted themselves unto the righteousness of God. For Christ is the end of the law for righteousness to every one that believeth. (Romans 10:1-4)

My People, the Amish

My People, the Amish

The Amish

The True Story of an Amish Father and Son

Joe Keim

ANEKO
PRESS

We love hearing from our readers. Please contact us at
www.anekopress.com/questions-comments with
any questions, comments, or suggestions.

Visit Joe's website: www.mapministry.org
My People, the Amish – Joe Keim
Copyright © 2017
First edition published 2017

Scripture is taken from the King James Version, public domain.

Cover Design: Natalia Hawthorne, BookCoverLabs.com
Cover Photography: Original cover photo by F. Robert Openshaw
Amish Father and Son: Abner Zook and his son Gideon
Writing assistant: Donna Sundblad
Editors: Sheila Wilkinson and Michelle Rayburn

Printed in the United States of America
Aneko Press
www.anekopress.com
Aneko Press, Life Sentence Publishing, and our logos are trademarks of
Life Sentence Publishing, Inc.
203 E. Birch Street
P.O. Box 652
Abbotsford, WI 54405
BIOGRAPHY & AUTOBIOGRAPHY / Religious
Paperback ISBN: 978-1-62245-445-7
eBook ISBN: 978-1-62245-446-4
10   9   8   7   6   5   4   3
Available where books are sold

Contents

I would like to first dedicate this book to my sweet wife and our children and grandchildren. You are God's most precious gift to me on earth. In fear and trembling, I have passed the faith on to you. Don't drop it. Fan the flames. Pass it on.

Secondly, I dedicate this book to all the fathers and sons who have worked so hard and diligently at working through relational struggles. God bless you!

Wherefore seeing we also are compassed about with so great a cloud of witnesses, let us lay aside every weight, and the sin which doth so easily beset us, and let us run with patience the race that is set before us, looking unto Jesus the author and finisher of our faith; who for the joy that was set before him endured the cross, despising the shame, and is set down at the right hand of the throne of God. (Hebrews 12:1-2)

Acknowledgements

For many years, I dreamed of writing a book about my life, but my fear of not being able to finish kept me from starting. One day I realized now was the time to write. I sat down at my computer and my fingers tapped away on the keyboard. In no time at all, I had typed twenty pages; but then it happened. The computer crashed and twenty pages disappeared into thin air. I threw in the towel and forgot the idea of writing a book.

After several years, Jeremiah Zeiset from Aneko Press, the publisher of my book, encouraged me to write my story. When I declined, he suggested collaborating with writer Donna Sundblad. So with weekly interviews, *My People, the Amish* has become a reality.

Thank you, Jeremiah Zeiset, for your continual encouragement throughout the writing and re-writing and for the many hours you invested in overseeing the entire project. You know how to make things happen!

Thank you, Donna Sundblad, for the energy and passion you brought out of me. I will forever be grateful for the Friday morning phone conversations as we laughed and cried all the way through my book. Thank you, Sheila Wilkinson, for the many hours you put into editing and proofreading. Thank you, Bob Openshaw, for traveling from California to Pennsylvania to capture the perfect photo for my book cover. I've been blessed by your friendship and generosity.

Abner and Gideon Zook, thank you for your willingness to become the father and son on my cover. Not only were you a perfect representation of me and my beloved father, but you enriched my spiritual life with your strong faith and ability to think outside the box.

Thank you, Natalia Hawthorne, for all the time you put into making the book cover pop, going out of your way to care about the tiniest details.

Thanks to my beloved wife, Esther Keim, for the numerous times you helped me brainstorm to get the story right. Thanks to my children, Jonathan and Rachel, son-in-law, David Garwood, and soon to be daughter-in-law, Havilah Justice, for the parts you played in the book. Each one of you brought perfection to *My People, the Amish.*

Last, but far from least, I want to thank Jerry and Carol Gess, Shawn and Debbie Strong, Brian and Rene' Budd for filling that important family void in our lives. Thank you Pastor John Bouquet for being our family shepherd for thirty years. Thanks to my brothers and their wives, William and Jenica Keim, Johnny and Miriam Keim, Perry and Maryann Keim, for all you do to stand with the ministry. Thank you, staff, volunteers, donors, missionaries, board members, and prayer warriors for your priceless partnership and servant hearts. Together, we have become a giant army in the Lord's work. Thousands of Amish people have given their lives to Jesus Christ because we chose to band together and stay faithful to the end. Soon we will rejoice from the labor of our work.

Prologue

I woke up with a start that Sunday morning. Church services would soon begin across the field from our house – the same place where Esther and I had exchanged our wedding vows nine months earlier. As we lay in bed, we talked about our decision and made last-minute plans.

"Joe, you're gonna have to let my parents know that we are not attending church today," she urged.

Hesitantly, I crawled out of bed and walked over to my in-laws' part of the house and informed them we would not be at the service that morning.

My father-in-law looked at me and said, "Then I'll stay home too."

That's not going to work, I thought. People were coming at 9:00 to help us move. "Okay, I'll go to church," I said.

With that, my father-in-law agreed to go. It was like Esther's parents knew something was up. I put on church clothes and took off walking across the field where others gathered. Esther stayed home to direct our friends in the move.

When I walked into the barn where the men were, my father-in-law acknowledged me and nodded his head as if to say he was happy with my decision. By 8:40 all the preachers started toward the house. Because Esther's dad was a preacher, he was in the first group to leave. I watched. At the moment I saw him enter the house, I turned and fled without saying a word to anyone. I ran out the back door, across the field, and into the house where friends were carrying our belongings to the truck.

They flung pillows and bedding out the upstairs windows to the ground below. Others rushed around, gathered our goods, and loaded the truck. It only took fifteen minutes to load all of our possessions.

Before we left, I wrote a note to my father-in-law and my parents to explain why we were leaving the Amish. I shook uncontrollably and cried bitterly. When I finished, I looked at the note. It didn't make sense, so I tore it up. I wrote a second note and then a third. I threw all of them away. With a gripping sorrow in my heart, I knew that anything I wrote wouldn't make sense to those we were leaving behind. I knew the immense hurt and pain I would bring my dad and mom again. I knew this would be the last time I would leave the Amish and I would never return.

Chapter 1

How I Became Amish

I grew up Amish, with the Jewish name Keim. While that may seem unusual, it's an example of how God orchestrates – how He arranges the pieces of our lives to create His story, or as we say, our history. For my story, we can trace those puzzle pieces back to the late 1600s when a Jewish man by the name of Johannes Keim boarded a ship and set sail for America. He landed in Germantown, Pennsylvania, in 1698, penniless and single at the age of twenty-three. He returned to Germany in 1701 and married in 1706. He and his wife returned to America in 1707 and established the first Keim home in Berks County, near Reading, Pennsylvania.

That Keim family gave birth to the first generation of American Keims. Their son John Keim grew up and had a family of his own. His son, Johannes Peter Keim, fathered three sons, but his wife died when the boys were young. The oldest of these three boys, Nicholas, was born February 2, 1768. After his mother died, his father was unable to care for him and his younger siblings. As a result, the boys were adopted by various neighbors. Young Nicholas worked for an Amish family and learned Amish ways early in life. He became part of an Amish community and the first Amish Keim – my ancestor.

We are able to trace my family's Amish roots back to Holmes County, Ohio, where my grandparents, William and Laura Keim, grew up. After they married and had a family, they decided to leave that area because, in my grandfather's view, the influence of the growing tourism trade left a more liberal Amish lifestyle in its wake. These liberal-minded Amish tended not to excommunicate and shun as much as my grandpa wanted, so he picked up his family of eight children, moved forty miles west to Ashland, Ohio, and bought a 200-acre farm. There they founded the Old Order Amish community that is still present today.

My father was a young teenager, fresh out of school and ready to be mentored and trained to someday own and operate his own business, which is a very common practice in the Amish culture. I know very little about my father's growing-up years, other than he was the second oldest child in the family. He seldom talked about his boyhood years, but once he said it was difficult for him to leave his friends and cousins when they moved away from Holmes County.

In his early twenties, my father was drafted and pressured to join the army headed to Vietnam. Like so many other Amish young men, he refused to fight in the war, so outside authorities arrested him and put him in prison for over a year. While in prison, he was often made fun of and belittled because of his beliefs, making it a difficult and trying time for him. Loneliness haunted him as he felt disconnected from his family and culture. I don't think Dad ever got over that part of his early years.

The new community in Ashland, Ohio, grew to several hundred families, and the groomed farmsteads belonged to what many who lived there considered an Old, Old Order, because my family was even more conservative than the Old Order in

Holmes County. As the first ones to move to Ashland, they came up with their own list of dos and don'ts, which Amish churches refer to as the Ordinance Letter. These rules were more conservative than their previous list and affected everything from dress code to buggies and even included their farming and houses. For instance, we weren't allowed to wear short-sleeves or have buttons all the way down the front of our shirts, because that was too worldly. Instead, we could have three buttons and no lay-down collars.

In Ashland, bigger head coverings were required for women compared to those in Holmes County, where the women might have three or four times the number of pleats, making the head covering appear much fancier. Holmes County coverings were smaller in size and allowed more hair to show in the front. For Ashland men, our hat brims measured three-and-a-half inches, while in Holmes they were an inch smaller. Again, the bigger the brim, the more conservative. And anytime we left the property, we had to wear those hats and bonnets. Holmes County Amish were seen running around without hats and bonnets in town, and for this and similar reasons, my grandparents left Holmes County behind and drew up the much more conservative Ashland Ordinance Letter.

The Ashland community grew quickly and spread into other counties. Amish seeking a more conservative group made the journey from various parts of the country, vowed to submit to the Ashland Ordinance Letter, and became members of the church. Quite a few hailed from the Holmes County area. They had large families, and as the families expanded, they celebrated weddings, and the number of districts grew.

Those who live in the Ashland community are proud to be considered even more conservative than the Old Order. Like I said, you can tell how conservative a community is by the style of their hats and bonnets, but even as you drive through an

Amish community and see the color of their curtains, you learn a lot about the community. For instance, in Holmes County, curtains hanging in homes vary from white to other light colors. In Ashland, we were only allowed dark blue or black.

In the year 2000, the thriving Ashland community lost a number of families due to a clash of Amish culture with state hunting regulations. The big issue was hunter orange. The Ashland Amish wouldn't even allow the orange safety triangles on their buggies, and the law for hunters required them to wear a certain number of inches of orange. The Amish stood their ground, believing bright orange was a worldly color and a stench in God's nostrils.

The law of the Amish often clashes with the law of the land, and many times, the law of the Amish wins. In some cases, this can be good, and in others, not so good. The Amish, like their Anabaptist forefathers, have a lot of zeal and determination. Numerous individuals have been fined, put in jail, and forced off their own properties over refusal to buy building permits, install fire alarms, and bring indoor plumbing up to code. The Amish believe that once they agree on a church rule and write it in the Ordinance Letter, it is both recorded on earth and in heaven. They use the conversation that Jesus had with Peter to support this: *And I will give unto thee the keys of the kingdom of heaven: and whatsoever thou shalt bind on earth shall be bound in heaven: and whatsoever thou shalt loose on earth shall be loosed in heaven* (Matthew 16:19).

Deer hunting in Ashland was by far the most exciting thing that happened all year. Many men and boys would team up in groups of ten or more and surround a wooded area. While half the team members started at one end of the woods, shouting and driving the deer through the woods, other team members would stand at the opposite end waiting to shoot the deer when they came through. Not only did we annoy our English neighbors, we also frustrated the game warden, who kept ticketing deer hunters for not wearing hunter orange. One year, the game warden was so upset and frustrated that he drove around the farmlands in Ashland County asking hunters to meet him on a certain day and at a certain time and place. When everyone showed up, he ticketed all of them for not wearing hunter orange. As a result, many Amish left Ashland so they could hunt.

But that wasn't the only reason families left. Bickering over little things grew into big issues over the years, which greatly saddened the remaining families and led them to reach beyond themselves for help. They invited wise men from other Amish communities to come and meet with their remaining families.

The meeting day finally arrived. The muffled clip-clop of horses' hooves and the hum of steel-rimmed buggy wheels marked the arrival of family after family. They parked their buggies and walked with grim expressions to an open meeting area in the upper part of the barn. The men and women sat on hard wooden benches, facing the wise ones, and slipped off their hats and bonnets. When the meeting came to order, the men asked members of the community to share the problems that brought so much heartache to this once active Amish community.

One after the other, folks shared from the heart. Some shared in anger, others in frustration and confusion. Finally, the last member had his say. When he took his seat, a hush fell over the gathering. Sparrows and pigeons chirped and cooed as they flew back and forth from one rafter to another, while the people waited for the wise men to get up and tell them where they had failed as a community.

Finally, one of the men, Jonas, stood and cleared his throat. He said, "Friends, listen closely. Your problem is not whether one should or shouldn't wear bright orange when hunting deer; neither does having or not having bulk milk tanks have anything to do with all the division and anger coming from this community." He waited a moment for his words to sink in. "All this confusion, anger, bitterness, and division could have easily been avoided if you had heeded God's command, when He said: *Thou shalt love thy neighbor as thyself* (Mark 12:31)."

They had lost their first love and their love for each other. As more rules and regulations were invented to control life, bickering and comparing of each other occurred. When I was a little boy, the Weavers, who were neighbors, came to our house to discuss church issues. My parents never told me what the issues were, but I do know the Weavers were very angry and determined to be heard. The meeting between my parents and the Weavers got so intense, I could hear them yelling at each other from another building. Many in the community had forgotten, or were totally ignoring, the teaching of the apostle Paul about their walk in Christ.

> *Blotting out the handwriting of ordinances that*
> *was against us, which was contrary to us, and took*
> *it out of the way, nailing it to his cross ... Let no*
> *man therefore judge you in meat, or in drink, or in*
> *respect of an holyday, or of the new moon, or of the*
> *sabbath days* (Colossians 2:14, 16).

Such disagreements and tensions cause divisions in many denominations, and the Amish are no different in this respect.

Chapter 2

Growing up Amish

Now that you know how I came to be Amish, let me tell you about who I am. My name is Joe Keim, the oldest of fourteen children. I'm named after my Uncle Joe. One of my brothers died when he was a couple of weeks old, so Dad and Mom raised thirteen children. While most Amish depend on a midwife during the birthing process at home, my arrival into the world was somewhat unique. I was born in the hospital. No one ever told me why, but I've always assumed my mom had some complications and needed to be in a hospital atmosphere in case something went wrong.

My hospital birth reminds me of a short story that, while fictional, sheds a little light on the Amish mindset.

> Grandma and Grandpa came to the hospital to visit their new grandchild. They arrived on the second floor and stood before a window where they viewed all of the newborns lined up so people could walk by and see their little faces. First Grandma and Grandpa tried to decide which one was their grandchild. At

the moment they found him, they separated him from all the others saying, "He's such a lucky baby. He could have been born into an English family, but God favored him by choosing otherwise. As soon as we get him out of this hospital, we will take him home and dress him in Amish clothes. He will learn the Amish dialect, attend Amish school, and learn Amish ways. When he is old enough, he will join the Amish church, marry an Amish wife, raise an Amish family, and die in his Amish clothes. If he follows through and does all this well, there's a good chance he will get to heaven."

As I grew older, more and more siblings joined the family. My parents never told me where babies came from. They just mysteriously appeared. Whenever a birth took place during the day, Dad and Mom would send us children out of the house, and when we returned, we had another newborn baby. On one occasion, they sent us out to strip the sorghum leaves. Sorghum is a tall cane that resembles field corn with a cone-shaped seed head filled with BB-sized seeds.

As each one of us walked out the door single file, my father gave strict orders, "Don't leave the sorghum field until I invite you back to the house."

We were clueless as to what was happening, and quickly followed orders. Hour after hour went by as we stripped leaves from one stalk after another. Our hands hurt and dirt covered the entire front of our bodies. Hunger pangs set in and time stopped moving. *Did our father forsake us? Did he forget?*

Suddenly, out of nowhere, Dad appeared with a huge smile on his face. "Come here," he said. "Mom and I have a surprise for you children."

As we followed Dad out of the field and toward the house, he built our level of excitement. We loved surprises and couldn't wait to see what it was. When we finally got to the house, Dad led us into the kitchen, through the living room, and all the way to our parents' bedroom. There was Mom lying on the bed with a tiny little baby by her side.

As we stared wide-eyed at our new brother, Mom simply said, "An angel dropped him off."

At this time in my life, I believed everything Dad and Mom told us. With all the excitement, I never thought to ask questions, but gladly took my turn holding our newest brother. I walked away wondering what the angel looked like. Did he have wings? How long did he stick around after dropping our little brother off?

As I got older, things began to make more sense. I started noticing that whenever Mom's waistline bulged, she stopped attending the bi-weekly church services. This happened about a month before another baby was "dropped off," but the word *sex* or even the term *having babies* was never mentioned.

I was about thirteen when I first heard about sex and where babies came from. I was hanging out behind the barn with some of my first cousins. Paul, my oldest cousin, knew more about this stuff than the rest of us, and he shared bits and pieces of what he had heard. We laughed hysterically. In fact, each one of us boys laughed and joked until the tears rolled down our cheeks.

I could go on, but you get the drift. My view of sexuality from the very beginning was twisted; at best, it was half-truth and half-lie. If a mature grownup had talked to me about this topic, the barnyard discussion would never have taken place the way it did.

Let me go one step further. If a mature grownup, specifically our parents, would have taken the time to sit down with each one of us at home and discuss the truth about sex and pregnancy, we may very well have looked at sex as the gift from God that it is. Rather than sex becoming a joke and a dirty word, we may have realized sex was something beautiful and worth waiting for until we got married. Instead, everything but that happened.

My Father

To say my dad was hard working is an understatement. He owned a blacksmith and machine shop, a vitamin and herb store, and also owned and operated a 200-acre farm. He wrote several books, and people, not just the Amish, considered him to be the community veterinarian and came to him for help. He even shoed show horses. In addition to caring for the animals, he served as the community dentist and pulled teeth for the Amish. But the thing he is probably most known for is the burn salve he invented. Most Amish households have a small white plastic jar of B&W Ointment in their medicine cabinets, and it's even used in some US hospitals. He has spoken at several hundred seminars and trained and certified hundreds of Amish people on how to apply his burn salve and use dried burdock leaves. As a result, he knows and works with many medical doctors and hospitals in the US.

My local chiropractor once shared how my father asked him to taxi him to an out-of-town doctor's meeting where more than one hundred medical doctors from all over the country had planned to meet. When they arrived, they got out of the car, walked across the parking lot, and entered the building.

"Joe, no kidding, we entered that room, and many of those doctors knew your father by his first name," he said. My chiropractor told how he stood in awe as he watched my father, the only Amish man in the whole place, walk around and shake hands with highly educated doctors and participate in deep, college-level discussions.

As you can see, to say Dad was a very busy man doesn't begin to cover it. With so many outside commitments, he didn't have a lot of time for his family, and I felt neglected – as if Dad's goals in life and his customers were far more important than me. When we did have time together, he often pointed out things we didn't do well enough. That was it. No time for real conversation or just talking about the day. Just enough time to let me know I didn't measure up to his expectations.

In my mind, he seemed frustrated and short tempered because he was so busy helping people outside of the family. Eventually, in my teen years, my feelings led to a disconnect between us.

Dad farmed organically, and his approach to good health was the all-natural approach. He strongly believed in vitamins and herbs and frowned on having any cakes or pies. However, Dad loved fruit, and around Christmastime he treated us to whole boxes of oranges and grapefruit.

We looked forward to Dad bringing home fruit, and sometimes Dad brought home pineapple, which is one of the sweetest fruits and has great medicinal value. Now, I know cleanses are all the rage these days, but I can tell you firsthand they are nothing new. Dad asked my whole family to go on a three-day pineapple diet because it would clean us out – "worms and all." While pineapples are deliciously sweet, they are very acidic. By the third day of a pineapple-only diet, my sore mouth burned with every bite. And we dared not eat anything but pineapple, because Dad wouldn't stand for it. At the time, it was NO laughing matter, but now I admit, it gives me a chuckle.

My Mother

Mom, on the other hand, was a very caring mother who loved us children unconditionally. I enjoyed a close relationship with her and often poured my life troubles out to her while she sat silent with a long-caring face that told me she really listened.

In the end, she always said the right words to make me feel things were going to be okay.

Mom was also a hard worker. Not only did she hand sew all our clothes and make us three meals a day, she also planted two large gardens, did all the fall canning, helped Dad in the shop, and lent a hand with the milking every morning and evening. We bought our butter and cheese from the man who picked up our milk, but Mom always made our bread. We seldom had pie or cake, though, simply because Dad thought these foods had too much sugar. This often raised contention between my dad and mom. Looking back over my childhood years, I wonder in amazement how she was able to do all she did. She was a gifted wife and mother.

Mom had a few breakdowns, which usually happened at night after we went to bed. On one of these occasions, my father woke us in the middle of the night and said, "Get up and come downstairs as quickly as possible. Mom is dying!"

Within seconds, we were all wide awake and ran to Mom's side. As we gathered around her side of the bed, we saw her struggling and gasping for one more breath of life. Her face was pale, and she couldn't even talk to us. We stood there, looking down at one of the greatest mothers of all time. My heart hammered so hard it felt like it was going to jump right out of my body. My chest ached from the pounding, and I felt totally helpless. We all thought this was it. Mom was going to die right before our eyes. Tears trickled down the side of my face, and my body trembled in fear. In unison, our family began to call out to God, asking Him to spare our precious mother's life.

Looking back at it now, I'm not sure why we didn't call an ambulance. It may have been because the nearest phone was owned by an English family, two miles away. It may have been because it was in the middle of the night and Mom seemed to be too far gone. In the end, Mom hung in there; within days, she started feeling better and going about her daily routine.

Family Life

When it came to meals, we had to eat what was set before us. Personally, one of the most difficult things to eat was soft-boiled eggs. Mom, at my father's request, boiled dozens of these eggs for three minutes on the wood-burning stove. It took a good thirty minutes to get the stove hot enough to boil eggs. They were then placed before us on the table, we stirred them into homemade breadcrumbs.

My problem was the chalazae. If you've never heard that word, you might know it as the slimy things, the whitish strands of goo that anchor the yoke to the center of the thick, white membrane. For me, that goo was the thing that made me gag. And the fresher the eggs, the more prevalent the strands. I'd stir that egg and breadcrumb mixture until I found every slimy strand, and when no one was looking, I picked them out of my bowl and smeared them on the board under the table where they stuck like glue and grew hard. Over time, they built up into a hard lump of plastered egg white slime, but at least I avoided the egg-gagging scene.

———————

Bathing in our family was not like bathing in English homes. We took a bath once a week on Saturday nights, which was the norm for the whole Amish community. When we were young, Mom heated the water on our wood-burning stove and poured the hot water into a long, galvanized tub. She'd add some cold water to make it comfortably warm, and a couple of children bathed at a time. With all the hard work around the farm in the summer, the water grew dreadfully dirty.

There's an old saying, "Don't throw the baby out with the bathwater," which comes from a time when everyone in the family bathed in the same bathwater once a year. The man of the house was first, then the mother, followed by the children, with the youngest going last. The water became so dirty it was opaque, which made it hard to see the baby in the bath. Well in my house, it was bad enough bathing once a week, even though we went swimming most summer evenings. The younger children bathed before the older, and by the time I climbed in the grungy gray water, I couldn't imagine how it could clean me; I hated being the last.

Sleeping arrangements with so many children also added an interesting element to life. While some of my younger brothers and sisters slept downstairs with Dad and Mom, most of us slept in the four upstairs bedrooms of our two-story farmhouse. The door at the bottom of the stairs was attached to a spring that automatically pulled the door shut in five seconds. Since we didn't have electric lights, we'd open the door all the way to light the stairwell enough to see. Then we'd race up the stairs as fast as we could before the door closed. Once that door clicked closed behind us, the hallway turned pitch black. From that point on, we'd feel our way through the dark until we got to our bed.

My father had taught us to kneel by our bedside every night and pray, and no matter how tired we were, we always prayed that God would watch over us. During the winter months, our bedroom temperature was so cold we could see our breath in the daytime. Snow leaked in through the edge of the small sliding windows and sometimes covered parts of the sill and edge of our bed. My brother Ervin and I would crawl under those ice-cold blankets and lie in bed with our backs turned against each other and cover up with heavy comforters that Mom had made for us.

Since there were twice as many boys as girls in our family, the boys claimed three of the four bedrooms. At the top of the stairs, you'd walk right into the first room. The oldest of my sisters slept in the room to the right, which had no door. A third room was farther around on the other side of the stairs, and the door to the left led to the room I shared with my brother Ervin. All of our beds were bought secondhand, and with so many children, we all had to double up in bed. Ervin and I were very close and slept in the same soft double bed that slanted toward the front.

During the summer months, we all went barefoot and most of the time Ervin didn't wash his feet. He often fell asleep before bedtime, and the mud caked on his feet dried and crumbled between the sheets. When I'd climb into bed, the springs and mattress creaked beneath my weight as I brushed and swept the mud crumbs away so I could sleep. But after working hard all day, I fell asleep within minutes.

Dissension Grows

I don't know if it's because I was the oldest or because it's what Dad expected, but I was a "goody-goody-two-shoes" kind of guy for the first fifteen years of my life. I never broke rules like some of the other children in our community, but always toed the line. At age fifteen, however, that all started to change.

Life for Dad was always black and white with no gray areas. His expectations and perfectionist personality for me as a young boy seemed unreachable at the time. As I transitioned from childhood into adulthood and went through hormonal changes, my voice grew deeper and my physical appearance changed. My mind dwelt on friends and girls much of the time. In the midst of all these big changes, I wanted to pull away from my parents, become independent, and make more decisions on my own. But I didn't have that freedom, and I certainly wasn't encouraged or guided in that direction. A simmering anger and resentment threatened to boil over within me.

Furthermore, Dad was very talented and was pulled in so many directions that he had little time to recognize the struggles of his eldest son. My mental and physical changes and his stressed lifestyle provided the perfect explosive mix. Looking back, I realize he was doing his best to bring me up with good morals and an honest, strong work ethic. But what I desperately longed for was encouragement and affirmation. I don't remember ever getting a hug from Dad or hearing him tell me that he loved me, but that's not uncommon in the Amish community. Most Amish people don't show affection. It's just the way it was. In fact, the word *love* isn't in the Pennsylvania Dutch vocabulary – the closest word for *love* is *like*.

When I hit my teens, my relationship with Dad deteriorated, so by the time I was fifteen, I often looked down at my feet when he gave me the day's work list. The work list was always verbal. The conversation was mostly one way – Dad telling us what he wanted done, and we took it from there. The frustration built in both directions. He was just as exasperated with me. One day when he met me coming around the barn, his body tensed. His frustration ignited and anger got the best of him.

"You are worthless. I don't even know why I feed you," he said.

What I wanted more than anything else in life was for my father to pat me on the back and say, "I know you are going through difficult changes in your life, but I love you just the way you are." I so desperately wanted my father to believe in me, even if he found it hard to do. I thought, *If my father treated me like he did his customers and cared about the things I cared about, life would be so much easier and satisfying.*

I understand it now. I was the oldest, and he'd never gone through this and probably felt he wasn't doing a good job as a parent, but at that moment those harsh words impacted my life. They completely shut my spirit down, and from that day on I gave up.

It saddens my heart to see so many Amish fathers raise their families on the harsh side, and this is even more profound in the ultra-conservative churches. They seem to have a harder time showing love and appreciation. Instead, rules are enforced and discipline is carried out more easily. When it becomes unbalanced like that, relationships can deteriorate very quickly.

Fathers, provoke not your children to anger, lest they be discouraged. (Colossians 3:21)

While my dad didn't have much time with me, somehow, he always seemed to know what I was up to. One time, when I was about fifteen, cousins were visiting from another settlement. They stayed at my aunt and uncle's house across the road from where we lived, so we went there to see them, and we were having a blast. When Dad said, "Time to go home," we didn't want to leave. But we did.

Ervin and I went straight to bed – or I should say we went straight to our bedroom. Our room had a window about the size of a pillow, and right outside the window was a porch roof that came within a foot of the bottom edge of the window. A very large oak tree stood right next to the porch, with branches that reached the porch roof. We slowly and softly slid the window open, trying not to wake our parents, who slept directly underneath us. My heart pumped faster as we crawled out the window on our stomachs and inched our way across the porch roof. We grabbed the biggest branch we could find and crawled all the way to the ground.

We bolted down our long driveway like lightning and across the street to my cousin Leander's place, where everybody was still awake. While the adults were busy talking in the living room, Ervin and I tiptoed upstairs. When we got to the top of the stairs, our cousins were shocked to see us, but excited that we had returned for more fun. We laughed and played, until from the corner of my eye, I spotted Dad! I froze. He had figured out what we had done and came looking for us.

The walk back to our house was a long one. Except for the noise of gravel under our feet, we walked in silence as we made our way back to our house. I knew we had done wrong. Our lane was a quarter mile long and it took a good ten minutes to walk from one end to the other. The walk down the lane gave me plenty of time to think about the spanking I'd get. We were headed to the barn, so I knew the spanking was a sure thing. Spankings often took place in the barn, a safe place, hidden from customers who came and went all times of the day and evening. As we walked toward the barn, Dad surprised me.

"This time, I'm going to have you spank me," he said.

You may be scratching your head at this, but let me tell you, it was a brutal punishment for my brother and me. When we entered the barn, Dad asked us to stay put until he retrieved the leather strap from another area in the barn. Neither Ervin nor I said a word as we waited in silence. We stood in a small circle of buttery light as I held the flickering kerosene lamp. From the darkness beyond, the sound of the cows chewing their cud marked time.

When Dad returned, he handed me the leather strap and said, "This time I want you boys to spank me."

He bent over the wooden, four-foot-tall feed box and waited. For several minutes, I stood there, unable to swing the leather strap. I didn't want to hurt my dad. Deep down, I loved him and wished we could talk this out. Several times he had to coax me on, until, with tears running down my cheeks, I halfheartedly swung the strap. Every fiber of my being wanted to flee. How could I hit my dad? This was a huge punishment for me, but that's what he wanted it to be. He wanted us to remember, and to this day I've never forgotten.

Spankings were a common punishment in our house, and they weren't just reserved for younger children.

One morning while we were milking, my dad said, "I'm going to spank you and you're not going to forget it."

I deserved this spanking like none other. I took off in a sprint. It took about three minutes to reach the house. I rushed through the door and dashed through the mudroom and into the kitchen by the time the screen door closed. I darted into the living room and up the stairs into my bedroom and then hastily slipped on multiple pairs of underwear.

As I pulled up the seventh pair, I looked up at the sound of footsteps. Dad stood in the door, his chest heaving, his stern face set like stone.

I screamed with all that was in me, "You can spank me, but if you do, I'm leaving and never coming back!"

For a moment, he stood there as if trying to figure out if a father should surrender to his oldest son's request. Just like that, my father turned around and left. I never got that spanking and the situation was never brought up again.

Chapter 3

School Days

In the Amish community, we went to eight grades of school. Amish schools all looked pretty identical – one room with a basement. The basement was equipped with a big furnace and was used to store wood and coal. The area immediately inside the door of the schoolhouse was known as the washhouse. Hooks lined the wall for our bonnets, hats, and coats, and above the hooks we placed our dinner buckets on a shelf. But the reason it was called the washhouse is because we washed our hands here.

Even without electricity, the room was not dark. Natural light filled the schoolhouse from big windows on three sides. Daylight shined in from the back of the room and from both sides. I don't ever remember getting there so early or staying so late that we needed a light.

Until we started school at age six, we only knew and used our Pennsylvania Dutch dialect. McGuffey Readers introduced us to English, and even though they were very simple books, they still set a clear ethical tone such as, "She is kind to the old blind man." In this way, as we learned to read English, the first

readers helped mold our moral mindset. While we were introduced to English from the start of school, we weren't required
to speak English until second grade. By required, I mean, at
that point, Pennsylvania Dutch was forbidden at school except
for during the lunch period. If we were caught speaking our
home dialect, we were punished. We would have to stand in
the corner, put our head down on the desk, or stick our nose in
a two-inch circle, which the teacher drew on the blackboard.

The seats in our one-room schoolhouse weren't all the same.
First and second graders had smaller seats, and as we grew bigger, the size of the desks changed proportionately. The desks
were all hooked together from the back of room to the front
desk. They weren't bolted to the floor, but to a two-by-four
wooden runner, which kept all the desks in tidy rows and still
made it possible to clean the wooden floor easily. School desks
provided us with a flat writing area and a small shelf to keep a
few workbooks, writing tablets, and pencils.

Our teacher sat in the center up front, and the blackboards
hung on the front wall on either side of her. Lower grades used
one side of the room and the upper grades the other. Large
alphabet cards bordered the wall above the blackboards at the
front of the room. Charts hung on the wall and were used to
keep track of our accomplishments. If we received 100 percent,
we'd get a star or sticker. It was a handy way to compare ourselves with others and challenge us to do the best we could.

Shelves along the side of the room held books, and we called
it the little library. It contained reference books such as the dictionary, but it also provided a small selection of reading books.
If we finished our work early, we could raise our hand and say,
"I got my work done; can I get a book?"

At this age, I didn't get in trouble often because I knew if I
got in trouble at school, I'd be disciplined at home too. The worst
trouble I remember getting myself into was the time a handful

of us made homemade cigars from corncobs. We drilled out the soft centers and filled it with corn silk. Then we hid behind the barn to smoke them, but got caught in the act. The teacher made me stay after school; everyone left but the teacher. The old clock kept time. Tick toc, tick toc. The teacher busied herself with paperwork. I sat – just sat. That was a long hour, and then I had to walk the mile and a half home by myself. For me, that was a killer – not having other kids to talk to on the trip home, but that was the worst discipline I ever received at school. To my surprise, I never got a spanking for this shenanigan.

The best part about school was recess. I could hardly wait for the buzzer to go off so we could go out and play. When the weather was nice outside, we played ground hockey, dodge ball, Andy over, kick the can, and softball. The church rules did not allow us to wear baseball gloves or play against sides like the professional teams. We caught all the fly balls with bare hands, which wasn't all that bad; however, about once or twice a year the softball would land on the tip of my middle finger instead of in the palm of my hands. And every time it happened, I'd scream out in agony and pain. The finger would swell up like a balloon and turn black and blue. For the next three or four days, it was nearly impossible to write with a pencil or milk cows.

During the winter months, we rode our sleds, made igloos, and chased each other with snowballs. Only when it rained did we have to stay inside during recess and play board games and three blind mice.

We didn't always have to walk to school. Because we trained ponies and had a mile and a half to school, we were allowed to ride our ponies. One particular morning, I decided to take a pony that wasn't ready to be ridden on the road. It was one of those times I knew better but did it anyway. I climbed on and the pony reared straight up, and I mean up – almost vertical. It lost its balance, came over backward, and fell on top of me.

It knocked me out for a minute or so, and when I opened my eyes, I saw Dad towering over me.

"Joe, you can't go to school."

I started to cry and told him I could go. I got to my feet, grabbed my dinner bucket, and ran up the lane toward the school, still crying because I would be late for school. I never missed one single day of school in eight years, and I took a lot of pride in that fact. It was a commitment I made to myself early in my school years.

Other than the times we were able to ride our ponies to school, we always had to walk. We trudged along that mile and a half no matter how hot or cold or in pouring rain. At times in the middle of our Ohio winters, I thought we'd freeze to death on the way home when the wind chill made it bitterly cold. We had one English neighbor who owned a pickup truck, and if he came along at the right time and found us walking, he'd pull over and lower the tailgate. As many as ten to twelve of us climbed into the bed of the truck, and he'd take us home and drop us off at the end of our driveways.

Chapter 4

The Holy Language

In our community, church was held every other Sunday. Communities were divided into districts with about twenty-five families per district, because that's all that could fit in a house. Once a congregation reached more than twenty-five families, they split into two districts. An average-sized community had five to six districts. Half the districts would have church one Sunday and the other half the other Sunday. This provided a way for families to visit another district on their "off" Sunday. If we stayed home on our off Sunday, the church made it clear, "absolutely no work on Sunday, except the morning and evening chores." Instead, Dad required us to read the German Bible, from after breakfast until noon.

At the time, we hated it. German was a third language and difficult for us to understand. Now when I look back, I see Dad did something most households didn't do. He gathered us into our sparsely furnished living room to read the Bible. Our couch looked more like a daybed because our community's rules didn't allow a back or side on our couch. Some communities allowed backs but no sides, and others allowed a whole sofa with back and sides, but our community only allowed the daybed style couch. Mom made multicolored coverings for the couch and rocking chairs.

As we gathered in the living room, the ambient tick of the old cherry grandfather clock whispered in the background. This mammoth clock reached from floor to ceiling like a sentinel marking time. Dad walked to the hutch that was on top of our slant-top desk. This is where we kept our prayer book, German Bibles, the *Martyrs' Mirror*, and other important books. He gathered us in a circle and helped us pronounce those German words, so we'd be able to read and understand the Bible. While he taught us how to read and understand the Bible in German, he often shared Old Testament stories. It was also during those family times that Dad warned us of the danger in the world outside of Amish communities. He taught us that the world would continually grow more and more wicked, just like Sodom and Gomorrah. In our young minds, we thought the Amish people were the only reason Jesus had not yet come back to end the world.

I praise God that Dad cared about the Bible and wanted us to read and understand it. We looked at the German Bible as a holy book, and for that reason, marking or highlighting any part of the pages was forbidden. We weren't even allowed to stack anything on top of it.

Not only was the Bible in German, but all the Amish church services were held in German as much as possible, because it was considered the "holy language." Some said German is the language spoken in heaven, and it was the language God used when He spoke to Adam. Some even say Jesus spoke German.

In all, we Amish knew three languages. We mainly spoke Pennsylvania Dutch, a dialect of German. We read and wrote English, and spoke it starting in the second grade. For High German, we had Martin Luther's translation of the Bible, our prayer book, *Martyrs' Mirror*, and our hymns – all in the holy language. This was the language we understood the least of the three we knew. In school and around home, we sang our hymns in German and read from German prayer books. And it seemed the more German the preacher used in his preaching, the more holy the service was.

The *Martyrs' Mirror* was a big book about three inches thick, which contained hundreds of stories and articles that were written about our forefathers in Switzerland. The stories described the severe persecution that went on during the early Anabaptist movement. Over four thousand men and women gave their lives in various ways to stand for biblical truth and freedom. Some were burned at the stake; others were beheaded; and some were tied up with ropes and drowned in rivers. The *Martyrs' Mirror* was very dear to us and in many ways was held to the same level as the Bible. Our German hymnbooks were just as valued. Many of the hymns were written by our Anabaptist forefathers while they were fleeing for their lives and hiding in caves. As you might imagine, the stories and hymns were a continual reminder of who we were and where we came from.

Our hearts and minds resonated with Scripture passages like Hebrews 11:37-38, where it says: *They were stoned, they were sawn asunder, were tempted, were slain with the sword: they wandered about in sheepskins and goatskins; being destitute, afflicted, tormented; (Of whom the world was not worthy:) they wandered in deserts, and in mountains, and in dens and caves of the earth.*

Amish ministers don't preach with a Bible in hand, nor do they follow an outline. Instead, they memorize a list of familiar Scriptures and quote them throughout their forty minutes of preaching time. Many of these Scriptures are taken from the book of Psalms and various parts of the Old and New

Testaments. Along with Matthew 5, some of the more popular New Testament scriptures were:

> *Take my yoke upon you, and learn of me; for I am meek and lowly in heart; and ye shall find rest unto your souls. For my yoke is easy, and my burden is light.* (Matthew 11:29-30)

> *Be ye not unequally yoked together with unbelievers: for what fellowship hath righteousness with unrighteousness? and what communion hath light with darkness? And what concord hath Christ with Belial? or what part hath he that believeth with an infidel? And what agreement hath the temple of God with idols? for ye are the temple of the living God; as God hath said, I will dwell in them, and walk in them; and I will be their God, and they shall be my people. Wherefore come out from among them, and be ye separate, saith the Lord, and touch not the unclean thing; and I will receive you, And will be a Father unto you, and ye shall be my sons and daughters, saith the Lord Almighty.* (2 Corinthians 6:14-18)

> *There is therefore now no condemnation to them which are in Christ Jesus, who walk not after the flesh, but after the Spirit. For the law of the Spirit of life in Christ Jesus hath made me free from the law of sin and death.* (Romans 8:1-2)

Clearly, some of these verses warn about mixing with the world, which was a theme in much preaching. It wasn't uncommon to hear stories of those who left the Amish and later tried to return but couldn't. It was said they stayed away too long and finally God gave them over to Satan. No one knew for sure who these former Amish were or where they originated. Their stories were passed from one generation to the next and shared repeatedly at church and in family circles at home.

An often-repeated story involved an Amish man who left the fold years ago. In time, he found himself on his deathbed. As he neared death, he started screaming out, "The flames of hell are all around my bed." Then the man started crying out to God, promising that if God healed him, he would go back to the Amish. Suddenly, the flames of hell died down, and the man got his strength back. He crawled off his deathbed and walked out to the Amish community he'd left years before.

He walked from house to house, checking to see if certain people were still alive, but he always got the same answer. "Oh no, that person has died long ago."

When the man finally realized that he wasn't able to make things right with those he had disobeyed and turned his back on, he hung his head and walked back out into the world, realizing he had waited too long to return and God had shut the door.

A second example is based on a letter. This letter was preached from, copied, and read in homes, with the hope that children would never leave the Amish church.

Dear Father and Mother,

Well, I don't know how to begin, but I've been wanting to write you for so long and never had courage. I should have written sooner, but I knew how much it was going to hurt after what I have done to you, so I thought I'd put off writing as long as I could stand it. You don't know how hard it is for me to write this letter, but I have to do it sooner or later. My husband keeps after me all the time to write to you, but it hurts. I have sinned and don't know if God will ever forgive me for what I have done.

I know I have done a terrible, terrible wrong to some out here when I left my home and church and got married, but I did. I guess there is nothing left for me to do but ask you and God for forgiveness. My conscience bothers me day and night, and I'll probably take it along with me to my grave.

There is not one day of the year that I do not think of you, dear Father and Mother, and I'm terribly sorry for what I've done, but that don't change things. I was afraid if I'd write and tell you, it would hurt you so that it would kill you.

If I could do it all over, I would be back home helping you with my feet under your table. Oh, but it's all too late now, and I have no one to blame but myself.

You taught us children right from wrong, but it seems we took the wrong. I am crying as I write this letter, and it so hurts me. I say prayers every night when I go to bed, hoping God will hear me.

I thought of you all at Christmastime, thinking how awful you must feel the way your kids are. I can never forget what Brother Harley said on his deathbed, "Where are my lost brothers?" I guess sisters as well. Oh, how terrible. Please, oh, please, forgive me folks and pray for me.

Chapter 5

Church Services

In my mind, services were long and boring, usually lasting from 9:00 a.m. to 12:30 p.m. As a result, I didn't like going to church.

At 1:00 we had lunch. First, the married men gathered in the living room to eat while the married women ate in the kitchen. While they ate, the single boys and girls, age fourteen and older, sat and fellowshipped. When the married people were done eating, all singles were invited in to eat. The boys sat and ate in the living room, and the girls ate in the kitchen.

This type of separation permeates the Sunday gathering. For instance, as a family we pulled into the driveway where church would take place that day. We dropped the women off at the house, and Dad and we boys moved on to the barn, unhitched the horses, and stood in line with the other men and boys. At about twenty minutes before nine, the ministers walked single file toward the house and sat on the ministers' bench. Next, the oldest man walked toward the house with the married males following him – all single file and in the order of their age. Finally, the single men followed, also in order of age.

When the last boy sat down, the bishop asked the men to remove their hats. The sounds of hat removal lasted for about ten seconds. It made a weird sound that rang through the whole house – almost like a wind coming in from the north.

During the service, women sat in the kitchen, and the men sat in the living room on hard wooden benches. The legs on these benches were easily folded together and moved by wagon from house to house. The older men sat on the front benches with their younger children, and the older teens and singles sat in the last two rows, behind the adults. In the kitchen, the women and teen girls were arranged in the same manner.

At fourteen, we were out of school, and in this teenage season of life, I no longer had to sit with Dad. I moved to sit in the back rows with the single young people – not an adult but becoming an adult. Ah, it was such a good feeling to sit next to all my friends instead of Dad and my younger brothers. I also liked the idea of sitting farther away from the ministers and older men who watched us with eagle eyes.

My buddies had already informed me that the boys in the back row all took naps during the service. *Wow!* I thought. That will surely make the long, boring church service go faster, and it did. The truth is, it was not all that uncommon to hear snoring sounds coming from some of the older men in the front benches. Every once in a great while, someone on the back row would lose his balance during a nap and fall off the bench. The following is a true story, as told by Gerald Hochstetler, of a young Amish boy who fell asleep in church.

Through the Eyes of Little Tobias, the Amish Kid

Little Tobias tried his best to be a good little boy, sit up straight, and listen to the sermon, but it was all to no avail. Eventually, nature would take over, and little Tobias would put his arms on his knees, his chin in his hands, and doze off. It was not humanly possible to stay awake.

It was during one of those times that little Tobias had the most embarrassing experience of his life. At this point, sleep and nature were in complete control of little Tobias. He had his head between his hands, his arms resting on his knees, and he had sailed off to Amish la-la land. In his happy Amish dreams, he was feeding Amish goats and Amish chickens and feeling good about the farm world around him.

Suddenly, as if the heavens were speaking to him, one arm slipped off his knee, which propelled his body forward, and he stumbled across the aisle and into Mrs. Detwiler's lap (Mrs. Detwiler was also known as Mamma Roly-Poly). Gone were the chickens, gone were the goats, and Tobias found himself in a house – in a church house – and in a roly-poly lady's lap! It was a soft landing, much too soft for comfort!

To say that little Tobias was awake at this point is a complete understatement. In fact, words cannot describe the embarrassment little Tobias felt at this point. A few giggles slipped out, as some of the other boys tried to keep from breaking out into laughter, but for the most part, all who were involved and on the scene did a good job of keeping things serious, as it ought to be in church. The good old preacher never missed a beat, and nobody ever talked about it.

Among the Amish, there are certain things you just don't talk about. When things fly out of control as they did that Sunday, and situations come along that are out of their control, they let it go!

It's like wise old Papa Yoder says, "Many times silence and time is the best remedy." The Amish know that misfortune can strike at any time, to anyone, at any place, and so they carry on. The goats must be fed, the cows must be milked, and little Tobias must be forgiven for sleeping in church.

I received my first wool hat for Christmas the year I turned fourteen. Most Christmases, because of the size of our family, we didn't get many gifts. We received practical gifts – things we needed, such as new gloves and, of course, the treat of fresh fruit, nuts, and homemade candy. But that Christmas when I received my hat was one of the most exciting Christmases of all. The first Sunday after Christmas, our church wasn't scheduled to meet, so I visited another church district, just so I could wear my new hat.

Turning fourteen was a big deal to me. I'd graduated from a stocking cap to a wool hat and enjoyed the freedom of sitting with the young unmarried people on the last bench. One Sunday we gathered at my cousin Leander's house, and near the end of the service, I really needed to go to the bathroom – number two. I thought I could hold it, but the service went on and on. I started to sweat. In my mind, I told myself, *You'll get through this.* The end of the service didn't come and didn't come. I clenched my muscles trying to hold back. Finally, I couldn't hold it anymore, and I let go.

It was awful. The smell was bad and wafted through the living room. I just sat there in that room full of men. The service went on as if nothing had happened, but I knew they all had to know what I had done. I was embarrassed as I just sat there waiting for the end of the service. Fortunately, Leander's place was right across the street, and when the service finally concluded I made a beeline home. I ran across the road and down the lane to our house. While I was changing clothes, my mom showed up. She felt so bad for me and comforted me. I didn't go back that day because I just couldn't face any of them. To their credit, no one ever talked to me about it. They just left it alone.

Choosing a Preacher

In the Amish church, our preachers are chosen by lot. Each district has its own bishop, deacon, and two lay ministers. We couldn't become a bishop unless we had already served as a deacon or lay minister. Deacons and lay ministers were chosen from the membership. When one of them moved away or died, the church voted on his replacement.

The making of a new preacher was always dreaded and made for a stressful day. Most men felt unqualified and considered the position to be very challenging. One by one, men and women walked into the bedroom to cast their vote for the man they thought would make the best preacher, and whoever received three or more votes was put into a lot. This usually consisted of six to ten men who were called out; they sat on a bench in front of those who had gathered. Each was handed a hymnbook with a string tied around it. Inside one of these books was a piece of paper. Whoever had the book with the piece of paper became the new preacher.

The men who got called out and asked to sit on the bench were common everyday people with an eighth-grade education. Most lacked knowledge of the Scriptures and had never spoken in front of a large group. When selected, many times the man started crying because it was a huge responsibility, and the only way out of it was to die. Often, the whole church sat with their heads down crying with them, until it sounded more like a funeral than a celebration.

All the people realized it was a big responsibility. After a preacher was chosen by lot, people of the community visited his house for the next few weeks to help the family with chores, from cleaning up manure to husking corn. What work they did depended upon the season. They offered this extra help to give the man time to study the Bible, because as I said, when Amish preachers deliver their message, they just get up and talk. This study time gave them time to memorize as many scripture passages as they could, so when they got up to preach they had something to say.

Some of these men can't preach, but they had to fill forty minutes. Sometimes, they ran out of things to say after ten minutes. As a little boy, I'd break into a sweat just listening to them struggle. I felt bad for them and prayed God would give them something to say.

Some years ago, the lot fell on an Amish man who responded with, "I can't preach."

But the rest of the ministers and members said, "But you have to preach. The lot fell on you."

Finally, the man replied, "Okay, I will preach."

After several unfruitful tries, he said it again. "I can't preach." This time he left the Amish and his family and turned to alcohol. After years of being an alcoholic, he finally died, separated from his family and banned from the church.

Casting lots is similar to tossing a coin or rolling dice. Before the Holy Spirit came at Pentecost, we see the casting of lots used seventy times in the Old Testament and only seven times in the New Testament.

> *And they appointed two, Joseph called Barsabas,*
> *who was surnamed Justus, and Matthias. And they*
> *prayed, and said, Thou, Lord, which knowest the*
> *hearts of all men, shew whether of these two thou*
> *hast chosen, That he may take part of this ministry*
> *and apostleship, from which Judas by transgression*
> *fell, that he might go to his own place. And they*
> *gave forth their lots; and the lot fell upon Matthias;*
> *and he was numbered with the eleven apostles.*
> (Acts 1:23-26)

Some, like the Amish, still believe it's God's way of revealing His divine will for the church. But some men don't appear to be called; what if they are not? Does this not put an extraordinary burden on a man whose calling is something else in life?

The eleven remaining apostles cast lots to replace Judas, and it fell on Matthias. But this happened before the coming of the Holy Spirit. Since the day of Pentecost in Acts chapter 2, God has done the choosing through His Spirit. Consider the apostle Paul: God stopped him in his tracks; He directly apprehended Paul and told him to go preach. We never hear any more about Matthias, but Paul's ministry encompasses most of the known world.

Neither are there any other instances in the New Testament where lots were used to determine church leadership. Instead, God gifted believers to serve in leadership positions and called them into ministry through the Holy Spirit.

> *And he gave some, apostles; and some, prophets;*
> *and some, evangelists; and some pastors and teach-*
> *ers; For the perfecting of the saints, for the work of*
> *the ministry, for the edifying of the body of Christ.*
> (Ephesians 4:11-12)

> *As they ministered to the Lord, and fasted, the Holy*

*Ghost said, Separate me Barnabas and Saul for
the work whereunto I have called them. And when
they had fasted and prayed, and laid their hands on
them, they sent them away. So they, being sent forth
by the Holy Ghost, departed.* (Acts 13:2-4a)

Some might argue that the New Testament church appointed men to serve as elders and deacons; however, that is not the same as casting lots (Acts 14:23; Titus 1:5).

Scripture aside, let's consider the Amish men who serve as ministers because the lot fell on them. God equips us for the work He has given us, but what if we are given a job we are not equipped for? Throughout my childhood, it was apparent that some were able to stand up and preach. It was just as apparent that others were not.

Chapter 6

Running

When I was fifteen, my cousin Eli ran away from home. He got his driver's license and bought a vehicle. At that point in my life, I believed anyone who left the Amish and became English would die and go to hell, so I wrote Eli a letter begging him to come home. The following is an excerpt from the letter that shows my desperate concern for my wayward cousin:

Oh Eli, please take heed today and not tomorrow because tomorrow it's too late. It's gonna be the Devil's day, and if he can't get you over the fence, he's gonna take you under it if he can. Oh please act fast. Oh please, you are my friend; please don't play with the Devil. I'm sorry that I ever done what I done. Just think; maybe you will be in a wreck, and then do you think you'd have a chance to go to heaven? Now if a good Christian had a chance of ten, you only got about one. I'm afraid the Devil's got you chained hard, and you can't ever get loose.

Now maybe if you came home, you'd only have to live

another four years [there]; compare those four years to hell that comes afterwards. Oh please remember as you go to work that hell will be here before you're ready. Oh please remember hell is forever and ever. Oh please come home. I'm praying for you and hope you're praying too. Remember hell – hell is forever and ever.

– Joe

On one occasion during this time, I walked to the outbuilding where we ground feed for the cows. I climbed up into the dusty rafters, laid down in the thick powdery residue, and cried and begged and pleaded with God that He would spare Eli's life.

Eli returned home and his parents tried to give him some options. He came to our place and Dad gave him a job working in the machine shop; the two of us became fast friends. By this time, he was eighteen and I was sixteen. Neither of us were happy; we talked about leaving the Amish and decided to do it together.

Just before I turned seventeen, before I went through with baptism, we made our break on a Sunday night. I wrote a note to my parents, and Eli did the same for his. We said, "We skipped the country. Don't come looking for us because you'll never find us."

I stole fifty dollars from my dad and took off, trying to run from the turmoil.

Eli had money in his pocket too, as the two of us hiked toward the city. We walked and walked and walked. About 4:00 a.m. we reached the city limits. Streetlights, neon signs, and, well, electricity lit everything up. We came to a street called Pleasant Street.

"Let's turn down this street," Eli said.

I was amazed at how close the houses were to each other.

We spotted an open garage door with two vehicles parked inside. Eli crawled into one, and I crept into the other. We were so exhausted from our long walk, we fell right to sleep. In the morning, the homeowner came out to go to work. When he discovered two Amish boys bedded down in his cars, he grew really angry. He yelled, "Get out! Get out of my cars or I'm calling the cops on you."

Half asleep and hungry, we headed back down Pleasant Street. In about an hour we got to the other side of town and came to a store called Big Wheel, which was like a Kmart. Before we headed into the store, Eli warned me, "They have big signs hanging from the ceiling with pictures of people's heads. They look through those eyes and watch you."

Sure enough, big posters with people on them hung from the ceiling, and just like Eli said, their eyes seemed to follow me wherever I went.

We walked into the Big Wheel with one thing in mind. We wanted to buy English clothes. At that time, the *Dukes of Hazzard* was a big deal. The T-shirt that caught our attention brandished a print of the Dukes flying up over a hill in their orange 1969 Dodge Charger. We each bought the same kind of T-shirt, a pair of jeans, and white tennis shoes. We paid, walked behind the store, changed into our new English clothes, and threw our Amish clothing into the woods – like dumping a body never to be seen again.

"Let's walk back downtown," Eli suggested.

We had no idea where we would live as we headed that way in our bright white shoes, new blue jeans, and our Amish hair-cuts minus our hats. To picture this, imagine how my dad cut our hair in a bowl-cut style. The hair had to cover at least half of our ears, and once our hair completely covered the ear, it was time for a haircut. That wasn't the rule in Holmes County where we came from though. They could show their whole ear, but our hair had to look identical throughout our community. So, there we were, two teens who were English dressed with Amish haircuts when we came across a porch sale. The lady sitting behind the table greeted us.

"Where you boys from?"

"We just left the Amish last night."

While we were on that porch rifling through the clothes and looking for some possible buys, a big van pulled up to the curb. It was loaded with Amish people. Among them was my mom. She spotted us. Less than twelve hours after we left our notes about leaving the country, I was found.

She climbed out of that van, marched up on that porch, and grabbed on to me and cried and cried and cried. I'm ashamed to admit it today, but I was very cold toward her.

"We're not coming back. All the begging won't do any good," I said in a wooden voice.

They finally left without us. That was hard. It shattered my world – and my mom's world.

The woman on the porch asked, "Where you staying tonight?"

We looked at each other and offered a shrug.

"Well, you can stay with me for just a couple of days. I have a spare bedroom upstairs."

To say we were relieved is an understatement. Even though it was only for a couple of days, that gave us a place to stay while we figured out what we were doing. What we didn't know was that her husband was in jail. When he found out his wife invited two men to stay with her, he made a promise to himself that as soon as he got out of jail he'd kill them both. Of course, we didn't know any of this was going on. We ended up staying with the woman for three days and became friends with another family who lived across the street. The Clantz family invited us to come live with them.

We moved in with the Clantz family, but my parents knew

where I was. The first time my dad came, he begged and pleaded for me to come home. I gave him the cold shoulder too. To my surprise, I woke up to find Dad still there. He slept on the concrete steps leading into the house. He did that several times. I ignored him. At sixteen and emotionally disconnected, I didn't feel my dad's love, and had no love for him.

One time, Dad met me in a busy parking lot in town. While Dad begged me to return to the Amish, cars drove by, coming and going, and suddenly Dad asked, "Can I give you a hug?"

I was shocked and couldn't believe what I heard. I'd never been hugged by him. There we stood, him in his Amish clothes, me dressed English. Awkward doesn't quite cover it. We were like two trees, stiff as a board, hugging each other. I mostly felt embarrassed, but deep down I also felt genuine love coming from a man I hardly knew, other than on the surface. When I refused to go home with him, he wept bitterly as he walked away.

From day one, Dad began to fast. Twenty days went by with no food. I thought a person would die after two weeks. Then three weeks, then four weeks. No food. Everybody knew my dad wasn't eating. Eli couldn't stand it.

"Joe, you have to go back. Your dad is going to die."

I refused.

One night Eli couldn't handle the thought of my dad going without food another day. He and one of the Clantz boys (Scott) said, "Get in the car. We are going on a ride."

The next thing I knew, they were driving me right out to my dad and mom's farm.

"Joe, you're staying here," Eli said. "If you don't, your dad is going to die. You're going to have to stay home."

I got out of the car because I felt I didn't have a choice. I slammed the door. Anger simmered toward Eli. How dare he do this to me!

Dad met me before I reached the house. He said, "I began to eat last night."

I wished Eli had known this. Dad went on to tell me how the night before, while in bed, he had a vision – not a dream. In the vision, a bright light shone from heaven onto his bed where he lay. He looked up through this light beam to the heavens and saw a pure white lamb walk out of darkness into the light beam. When it got to the center of the light beam, it turned its head and looked down at him. He knew right away it was Jesus. The lamb looked down for a time and then walked into the darkness again, and my dad snapped out of it. Following that vision, he had assurance all would be okay.

So here it was the day after Dad started eating, and sure enough, Eli dropped me off. It seemed really weird. When I walked into the house, all my brothers and sisters stood around staring in disbelief at their oldest brother dressed in English clothes and wearing an English haircut. I'm sure they were relieved that I had returned and wasn't going to go to hell.

Mom and Dad reached out to me, trying to understand why I did what I did. Dad even made a few promises about neighbors that had said and done things to me that were uncalled for. He shared how he had met with them and discussed their wrong actions. They in turn made promises to Dad that things would change, and they would be kinder toward me. But that only lasted a short time before life was back to normal – very busy, long hours, and no real emotional connection to those closest to me. I stayed home a couple of months, and then I left again.

This time, Dad visited the juvenile court judge, Judge McKinley, and talked to him about what he should do. The judge decided he would help Dad out and came to meet me at the Clantz house. After an hour-long conversation, he ordered me into the back seat of his car and took me home. He pulled into the driveway and got out. I, on the other hand, stayed in the back seat. The whole family gathered around the car, but I refused to get out. After coaxing and begging, I finally crawled out of the car. I was right back home but filled with anger.

Working part time on the farm and part time in my father's machine shop became a daily routine for me. But as time went on, my mind drifted back to the English world. I missed the freedom of turning on country music, living in an air-conditioned house, using the car for transportation, and yes, even the handy little electric light switches and outlets on every wall in the house. Another few months went by, and I ran away from home again, back to the Clantz house for the third time. This time I stayed away for three months. Dad decided to lay off me and stayed away for the most part.

While I had returned to the Amish several times, Eli remained English. In time, he made enough money at his job and was able to get a car and his own apartment. He also became involved with drugs and alcohol, and most weekends, he and I hung out together.

One time when partying with Eli, we smoked marijuana while driving in the country. I took a hit of marijuana and held it in as long as I could. Suddenly, it came to me that I was dying. I couldn't hear myself breathe, and it scared me.

Another night while I was English, we were having a party at a friend's house. That night I decided I was going to drink as much alcohol as I possibly could, hoping it would help me get over the fact that I was missing my family back home. Sometime during the party, I decided to take the stairway to a lower level in the house. As I stepped out at the top of the stairs, I lost my balance and fell headfirst down the long flight of stairs.

My cousin Eli rushed from the kitchen and came to my aid. He made me sit on his lap at the kitchen table, checking to see if I was okay. This is a perfect example of the colliding of the two worlds in which I lived. I sat there and cried. My life was messed up and miserable. I could see it happening but felt help-less to do anything about it.

One day in the winter, an Amish guy by the name of Andy called me from the home of an English man he was doing some carpentry for.

"I'm working out here," he said. "If you have a way, I'd love to sit down and talk with you. I want to try to understand what you're going through."

No one was home at the Clantz house, but the keys to the car hung on the wall. I had no license, but I swiped the keys and headed out to the car. I put that key in the ignition and started driving. I drove out to the country to see Andy, who would later become my brother-in-law. We sat and talked for a long time. Andy was easy to talk to and seemed to understand my life. It felt very good to get it all out.

Finally, I said, "Andy, I miss my family and friends, but I'm not going to come back to the Amish."

By the time I climbed back into the car, it had started to sleet. About a mile from the Clantz house, a truck slowed down to turn. I tried to brake on the icy road, but to my horror, the car slid. The next thing I heard was a loud crash. It all happened so fast. I slammed into the back of the truck. Within minutes, cop cars surrounded me. Police accused me of stealing the car because I didn't get permission to use it.

The cop said, "Your choice – detention center or back to your parents?"

Scared and shaking all over, I chose to return to my par-ents. So they drove me home. I got out of the squad car without hesitation, but for my parents and family, all this was getting a little old.

Chapter 7

Baptism and Joining
the Amish Church

In the Amish church, baptism and church membership happened on the same day. But to get to that day, the church required future members to go through three months of preparation, much like catechism classes in some churches. In our community that process began the year we turned seventeen. To start at an earlier age was forbidden. To start later meant you were a rebel.

The year I turned seventeen, my father arranged a meeting with me to discuss baptism and church membership.

"Mom and I are excited and looking forward to you beginning the baptismal classes this spring," he said.

"Dad, I'm not so sure I'm ready to take the step," I replied. "But I will spend some time considering it."

Seeing their child follow the footsteps of our forefathers was a parent's greatest dream come true. The pressure was significant. I didn't want to let my parents down, and I knew if I didn't begin classes, the entire community would classify me as being disobedient to my parents, my forefathers, the church, and God.

The problem for me was that I didn't feel ready. It mostly had to do with the fact that before baptism, I was under my parents' authority. If I acted up or did anything out of line, my father and I dealt with it, one on one. However, that would all change after my baptism day. From then on, I would have to give account to the preachers and church body. I already knew I couldn't live up to their rules, and whenever I didn't, they'd make an example of me in public. Even with all the pressure to meet everyone's expectations, I wasn't sure I was going to go through the process.

Decision day arrived far too quickly. Depending on what I decided, my life would be changed forever. As I jumped on my buggy and headed out the driveway toward William Weaver's place where church services were being held that day, I thought of all the rules we had to follow in the Amish culture. And here I was about to make a decision that would include making a vow to God and the church that I would never leave nor forsake the Old Order Amish church. It was all part of the membership package.

As the congregation began to sing from their hymnals, the bishop stood to his feet and left the living room to go upstairs. The deacon and two lay ministers followed. Now it was my turn to get up and follow the ministers to my first baptismal class. Elmer Weaver, who sat next to me, elbowed me in the ribs.

"Please, Joe, go with me. I don't want to go by myself."

Any other year, there'd be at least six to eight seventeen-year-olds going through membership class, but this year there were only two of us – Elmer and me. The two of us weren't that close, but we did have one thing in common; we went through eight years of school together.

Elmer stood to his feet and headed toward the door that

led upstairs where the preachers sat waiting. At that moment, I felt like a puppet with someone else pulling the strings. I got up and followed.

We sat in a circle: the deacon, two lay ministers, the Bishop, Elmer, and me. The Amish have eighteen articles of faith, and we had to go over each one of them before we could be baptized. Since we only met every other week and they went over two articles at each meeting, it took nine weeks. The problem for me was that all eighteen articles were written in German, and I didn't understand it well.

Our forefathers drew these articles up generations ago, and as I figured out later, they contained many scriptural truths. The problem in preparing for baptism was that the main focus wasn't so much the articles of faith as it was being challenged to submit and align with the ordinances of the church. During our nine weeks of training sessions, the membership was to keep a close eye on us. If any part of our lifestyle didn't measure up to the church standard, the membership was to report it to the deacon, who would in turn bring it to our attention. I failed miserably.

The deacon stopped by to talk to me throughout the week. I had bent the rim of my hat and decorated it to make it look like a cowboy hat. He said, "We cannot take you into the church and baptize you if you don't straighten your hat out."

So, if I wanted to become a part of the church, I had to change my hat back.

When I turned seventeen, Dad bought me a black horse named Mike and encouraged me to build my own buggy from the ground up. The horse and buggy would be used as transportation to go to the Sunday night singings and to take girls home for a date. Dad and I took a day off work, hired a taxi driver, and traveled to Holmes County, where we shopped at various buggy shops to buy the proper items needed to get started: shafts, axles, wheels, oilcloth, upholstery, paint, etc.

Over the next two months, I worked on my buggy every chance I had. Eventually the day came when everything was done except one thing. I still needed to paint the buggy black. As I stood in front of my buggy, feeling good about my accomplishments, an Amish man from the neighborhood walked in. The first thing he did was pull a tape measure out of his pocket and check the height of my front dash.

He looked around and said, "Joe, come over here. I just checked your dash and found it to be fifteen inches in height; according to our church ordinance letter, the dash cannot be any higher than fourteen inches. Yours is one inch too high."

I couldn't believe this man had the nerve to check my work, much less tell me I was one inch off on the height of my dash. He was the kind of church member who would go straight to the preachers and rat on me. If I refused to fix it, the church leaders would make it public to the church membership, and it would stop me from getting baptized. After talking things over with my dad, we decided I could either shave one inch off the top or tear the whole front end of my buggy out and rebuild the dash. We decided on the latter.

At seventeen years of age, it didn't make sense to me that I had to tear the front end of my buggy out over a dash being one inch too high. Liberal Amish communities have higher buggy dashes and, in some cases, windshields. According to the thinking in our community, lower dashes meant more humbleness, but this type of nitpicking over an inch played a role in driving me to leave the Amish community.

Blotting out the handwriting of ordinances that was against us, which was contrary to us, and took it out of the way, nailing it to his cross. (Colossians 2:14)

Another time, I drove my buggy to the gathering, and someone pointed out that I'd installed the wrong upholstery. I had used soft, brown upholstery, and it had to be replaced with black vinyl upholstery right away. I couldn't complete my baptism and membership until everything lined up with the ordinances. As a result, Elmer's and my baptism kept getting postponed.

Finally, we met with the ministers one last time, and they said, "Tomorrow we will ask you these questions and you will answer yes to each one."

The following day, people filled the barn. Next to a wedding, being baptized into the Amish church is the most attended event. Every parent and church wants this for the individuals, and at the time I thought it was what God wanted.

The church services that day were similar to any other, except at the very end Elmer and I were asked to kneel and make four vows to God and the church. The Bishop asked, "Do you believe Jesus Christ is the Son of God?"

"Yes, I believe Jesus Christ is the Son of God."

And I did, but my belief in Jesus Christ was a mechanical head knowledge that didn't reach my heart. It was just part of the extensive list of other things I was taught to believe.

Then the Bishop asked, "Can you renounce the devil, the world, and your own flesh and blood?"

I answered, "Yes, I can renounce the devil, the world, and my own flesh and blood."

"Can you commit yourself to all the ordinances of the church, according to the Word of the Lord, and be obedient and submissive to it and help therein?"

I said yes.

"Can you commit yourself to God and His church and abide by it and live therein until you die?"

Again I answered yes.

Making a vow to "commit yourselves to God and His

church" meant the Old Order Amish church I was about to be baptized into.

Now that I had made all four vows, the Bishop poured water on my head three times while the deacon used both of his hands to create a funnel for the water to land on the center top of my head. Afterward, the Bishop kissed me with a holy kiss. If a girl was getting baptized, the Bishop's wife would have given her the holy kiss. I had been informed by the preachers during membership class that as the water ran down over my head, it would wash away all my sin. I truly believed them. I got up from my knees as a member of the Amish church, believing all my sins were gone. I felt lighter. If I died on the way home, I'd go straight to heaven. Or so I thought. Later, I learned that while I got wet, that was it – nothing more happened to me that day.

Forasmuch as ye know that ye were not redeemed
with corruptible things, as silver and gold, from
your vain conversation received by tradition from
your fathers; but with the precious blood of Christ,
as of a lamb without blemish and without spot.
(1 Peter 1:18-19)

Chapter 8

Life and Death

As we were growing up, Dad found ways to keep us busy. Because we practiced organic farming, we didn't use any chemicals on our crops, but this created a tremendous amount of extra work for us boys that other farmers in the neighborhood didn't have to be concerned about. When Dad sent us out to pick mustard plants, I'd scan the field filled with thousands of plants bearing dainty yellow flowers and think, *We'll never get done!* Tears trickled down our cheeks in silent protest as we plucked each little stalk. We hated it so much, but we did it – for years.

We also harvested corn, and our twenty to twenty-five acres took a long time to gather. We husked by hand using a corn-husking hook. The job took a couple of months and sometimes ran into the winter. Even though I wore gloves, they got soaked and the cold bit into my fingers. I also wore this leather thing strapped on my right hand; then I pushed the hook along the husk to reveal the ear of corn. Once the husk was peeled back and the ear of corn was in plain sight, we'd break the ear of corn off and throw it on the wagon one ear at a time.

At the beginning of the season, it looked like an impossible task to finish, like moving a mountain one shovelful at a time. What made it harder on us was that our English neighbors with their big combines could husk an entire field of corn in one day, while we worked by hand one stalk at a time. As youngsters, the job seemed so big, but with so many of us, we often ran two wagons at a time and worked four rows at a time. Up and down, up and down, until we reached the last row in the center. Each wagon of corn was hauled from the field to the corn crib where we hand shoveled the ears of corn onto a gasoline-powered elevator. The chain-linked pads carried the corn up the elevator and into the crib. Every fall we loaded those cribs full of corn. Throughout the next year, we fed the cows and horses by emptying the corncribs one shovelful at a time.

Wheat and oats were usually cut during the hottest time of year. First, we'd pull the horse-drawn binder around the edge of the field. The binder cut the grain stalks about three inches from the ground and threw them into a binder web made of canvas. The web and gear contraption then moved the grain and stalks farther into the binder where rollers formed a sheaf, wrapped a piece of twine around it, tied a knot, and threw the sheaf on the ground. We usually started early in the morning and by evening sheaves lay scattered over the field.

After the milking and chores were done, our whole family went out to the field and began the long haul of picking up every sheaf and building what we called shocks. This task would often take us into the night, sometimes until after midnight. First, we'd stand two sheaves together like a teepee. Next, we set up others around the first two, leaving a hole to let the wind dry it from the inside out. On top of this shock we bent the last sheaf as a cover to keep the rain out. We did all of this by horse and manpower. We shocked all our wheat and oats and put loose hay up. In spite of all the work, the smell of fresh cut hay is still one of my favorites.

We had one threshing machine that we pulled around to help the neighbors, and while we were allowed to have a hay baler, we always put the hay up loose. The straw was blown into the huge barn and completely filled the large upstairs area, which we called the straw shed. We used this straw for bedding the animals and that kind of thing.

Having Fun

Looking from the outside in, one might think Amish life to be much like the old adage "all work and no play makes Jack a dull boy," but even though our entertainment options were few, some of the things we did for fun took up a great deal of our free time. For instance, we loved to go trapping. We'd spend months getting ready for trapping season. We'd boil the traps over a fire pit, pull them out of the pot, dip them in wax, and hang them. We spent the first day of trapping season setting traps for muskrats, fox, and coons. As a bonus, we were allowed to keep the money we made from any pelts we sold, which we usually put right back into trapping.

We also enjoyed hunting rabbits, squirrels, and deer – deer hunting was huge. And as soon as the season was over, we started planning for the next year.

We loved the outdoors and didn't just hunt and trap animals. We enjoyed them as pets, too. We had crows, coons, rabbits, and even a skunk. Crows were my favorite. Today my ears are still tuned to hear them as they're feeding their babies. That's the sound we listened for as children. It meant we only had a few days, because baby crows grow so fast. With an armful of short two-by-fours, a bag of twenty-penny nails, and a hammer, we walked the woods in search of the nest. When we located the tree with the crow's nest, we created steps similar to a ladder by nailing the two-by-fours to the tree trunk. This helped us get to the first limb. The nest was often nestled high up into the trees, so we climbed the limbs like sure-footed acrobats, stretched to reach the nest, and snatched the babies. Nests usually had just one or two baby crows.

We took them home and fed them egg yolks. The baby crows grew quickly and made good pets. All summer, they flew around the farm, landed on our heads, and lived in the house with us. Some of our pet crows learned how to pronounce words like a parrot. But in the fall, they traveled farther and farther away from the farm. As soon as this started, we had to clip their wings, or they would rejoin the wild and never come back.

Other fun pastimes included swimming in the summer and playing hockey in the winter when the ponds froze over. We made our hockey sticks out of pine wood so they'd be as light as possible. During weekdays, we would hurry and finish up chores as quickly as possible. By 8:00 p.m. we were headed for the pond with half a dozen gas lanterns, our hockey sticks, and shovels to clear snow off the ice. Within the next hour, boys from all over the neighborhood showed up and the hockey games began. With the intensity of professionals, we played until midnight. By then we were totally worn out and headed back home. Twice, someone fell through the ice and plunged down into twenty-five feet of ice-cold water. One time, my cousin Eli almost didn't survive. We had always been told that if a person came up and went back down for the third time, he wouldn't live. Eli went down for the third time before we could get a grip on him and pull him out of the ice hole.

In the summertime, those same ponds became our swimming holes. We were all great swimmers, and hardly a night went by that we didn't go swimming in someone's pond. During the day we worked, but as soon as the chores were done, all of us boys headed for the pond. It didn't matter that our cows and horses drank from the pond water, nor did it matter that fish, turtles, and sometimes snakes swam in the same water. Many times, darkness would settle in, and we couldn't even see each other's faces – just splashing, laughter, and lots of fun.

Working for the English

Until we were twenty-one, we had to give regular job earnings to our father. But we were always trying to find ways to make extra money, because if we helped our neighbors with a project and were paid, we were allowed to keep the money. One day, it occurred to us that we could train horses for English people. Dad was already shoeing their horses, which gave us numerous connections with his customers. Before long, word got out that the Keim boys were in the horse-training business, and English people started bringing their horses and ponies to us, so we would train them to be ridden. We had a lot of fun training them, and it made for some extra money in our pockets.

One day, an Englishman came to us and said he was looking to buy pigeons for dog-training purposes. He said, "I will pay you boys fifty cents for every pigeon you capture and bring to me."

Our eyes lit up, and so did our bank accounts. That summer we traveled ten miles in every direction and cleaned out every barn in the neighborhood. By the time we got done, there were hardly any pigeons left within a twenty-mile radius.

One night during that time, a handful of us went to an Amish neighbor's barn to catch pigeons and found out they'd just filled the haymow. It was so full we could walk across the top of the hay and grab the pigeons from the rafters. The problem with such a full haymow was that I couldn't see the two-by-four structure that ran down through the center of the hay like a frame to keep it from collapsing. This framework created a hay hole that ran all the way from the haymow to the concrete floor in the barn below. It was so dark I didn't even see the hay hole and I stepped from the hay into the opening and fell three stories. I hit the concrete floor in front of the cows in their stanchions.

The fall knocked me out, and I woke up with a big bump on the back of my head and a little blood. I got up and just went home. To this day, that hairless bump is still obvious on the back of my head and serves as a continual reminder of when I fell three stories and survived. I've always believed that Satan wanted to kill me that night, but God had other plans and wouldn't allow it.

Building a Go-Kart

When I was about sixteen, my brothers and I found out Dad was going to be gone for a week. We'd always wanted to build a motorized go-kart, and this seemed like the right time to do it. We all got our heads together and drew up the plans for the go-kart. As soon as Dad left, we took four wagon wheels, fastened them to an axle, and attached them to a wooden platform that measured two feet wide and about four feet long. Next, we cut a slot in the wooden platform, right above the rear axle. We added a pulley on the rear axle and hooked a V-belt up to a little Briggs & Stratton motor right above the axle. The front of the go-kart steered like a wagon, so we steered with one arm and pulled the motor down with the other to tighten the belt.

Finally, we were all done and ready to try out the homemade apparatus. Excitedly, we pushed it out from behind closed doors and lined it up with the driveway. Since I was the oldest and the go-kart was my idea, my brothers let me go first. I grabbed the steering handle with my left hand; with my right hand, I reached back and pulled the running gasoline-powered Briggs & Stratton forward. At first, the V-belt smoked like crazy, but once the go-kart was moving, it was all glory. I shot out the gravel driveway at about ten miles per hour – with no brakes.

As I got close to the end of the driveway, I slowed down just enough to round the corner. From there on, the road widened and was paved with asphalt. The noise of wheels and gravel died down, and my ride became much smoother. Little by little I doubled my earlier rate of speed to about twenty or thirty miles per hour. But then it happened.

I hit some loose gravel along the side of the road and lost control. In the blink of an eye, I found myself lying flat in the ditch, doubled over in pain, and my go-kart upside down smoking like a brush fire.

My brothers came running, wondering if I made it out alive. We quickly turned the kart over and cleaned all the dirt and gasoline away. Soon we had the Briggs & Stratton back up and running again. For the next several days while Dad was away, we drove that thing all over the place.

To this day, my English neighbor talks about it. He says, "I stood at my window and laughed and laughed at these Amish guys out there with this little motorized vehicle."

Looking back on the experience, I'm surprised we didn't break our necks, but we had so much fun, and I don't remember ever getting into trouble for it.

Contact with the English

We were so separated from the English culture that we seldom entered their houses. For my non-Amish readers, I want to take a moment to explain why we called non-Amish people *English*. It's simple; they spoke the English language. We grew up speaking an unwritten dialect of Pennsylvania Dutch, which is our mother tongue that we used to communicate among ourselves. We didn't learn English until we started school at age six.

I remember being invited to an English house one time. They made popcorn and showed us slides of when they went to Israel, but the thing that really caught my attention was the carpeting under my feet. *Oh my, how nice it would be to have carpeting*, I thought. But at our house that would be against the church rules.

At times, English customers who came into Dad's shop brought us candy. My all-natural, organic Dad wasn't happy about it. Once, he ended our sweet treats and made us dig a hole and bury the candy. Big wet tears fell to the ground as we obeyed him. I don't remember going back and digging it up, but I remember how mad it made me. *What's wrong with having candy?*

Our family made homemade ice cream quite often, but oh for the store-bought variety! Every once in a while, an English customer surprised us with several half gallons of store-bought Smith Dairy ice cream. What a special treat for all of us. Since we didn't have an electric freezer to store the ice cream until suppertime, the whole family immediately stopped working and gathered around the ice cream boxes with spoons in hand. We ate right out of the boxes.

One day an English tobacco chewer came along and three of us older boys accepted one leaf of Red Man tobacco and chewed it. Within minutes, we became very dizzy and got sick – very sick. All three of us went and lay under the shade of the big elm tree, sick as dogs.

One of my biggest early adventures into the English world happened on an Amish holiday we called Pinkst Mundog. This holiday was celebrated fifty days after Easter. On this one day in the year, everybody went fishing. We often teamed up with cousins and other friends in the neighborhood. This day, my cousin Eli and I said we were going to the lake fishing, but instead, we went to Kmart. Going to town hardly ever happened. I didn't even know how to get to Kmart, but Eli was a little older and knew the way. Regrettably, I stole money from my dad's cash register to spend. We bought battery-operated watches, a toy car with a racetrack, and a camera – all forbidden by the church rules.

While we were there, Dad came to town. We were so engrossed in our illicit activities and enjoying our freedom that we didn't see him walk into Kmart, but he saw us. However, he didn't say a word to us, neither did he show himself. We never knew he was there until later that evening.

As we headed back to the community, we had so much fun with that camera. We took countless pictures and played with our toys and battery watches. Before we got all the way home, we agreed on our cover story. "We'll say we fished all day and didn't catch anything. But we had a good time."

That night, my family gathered around the table to share favorite fishing stories of the day. Who caught the biggest fish, who caught the most fish, and who got the wettest? When I offered my cover story of how Eli and I had a few nibbles but no good bites, everybody was saddened that we didn't catch any fish – all except Dad. He waited until everybody was in bed, and then he told me how he'd made a trip to Kmart that day.

A sinking feeling churned in the pit of my stomach before he even said that he saw us. Needless to say, Dad was very upset. Today I only have a single picture left from that day. I have no idea what happened to the rest, but Eli and I sure had a lot of fun.

Leander

My cousin Leander lived across the road from our house. We were best friends from childhood up, so every chance we had, we played together. We played ice hockey, went swimming on summer nights, and set traps for wild animals. During the school year, we walked the mile and a half to school together and talked about everything and shared many secrets.

During the summer months, Leander and I spent many Sunday afternoons searching for arrowheads. We sold these to an English man in the neighborhood for five to ten dollars, depending on the size and condition they were in.

We also collected bird eggs from all the different birds in our part of the state like some kids collect rocks. To save the shell, we used a small metal pin to poke a hole in each end of the egg, and then we blew the yolk and white of the egg out the opposite hole. That way, the egg wouldn't spoil. I think we had about fifty different types of eggs in our collections. If one of us had an egg that the other one didn't have, we would trade. We placed them between dividers in a homemade shoebox, cushioned with soft cotton.

The two of us loved to ride our ponies together on Sunday afternoons and often raced them at high speeds. It wasn't uncommon for us to get dumped off, but we never got seriously hurt. Leander and I shared everything. We even fell in love with the same girl – Lydia Byler.

When I was seventeen and he sixteen, the two of us spent many nights camping out in our homemade teepee, which sat just inside the edge of the woods near a pond we used most often to play hockey and go swimming at night. For several years, we had been jumping from a tree limb into the water, but it was so high up that our heads really took a pounding by the time we hit the water. If we accidently belly-flopped, the impact knocked the wind out of us.

Finally one day, Leander said, "Let's build a real diving board."

We cut and carried four round posts and two-by-twelve lumber all the way back to the pond and built a diving board. We were so excited and couldn't wait to use it.

A few days later, Leander and I met up after the chores were all done and went swimming, enjoying our new diving board. Like so many other nights, when we finished swimming, we walked a few thousand feet into the woods and slept in our full-sized teepee. Within minutes, we were sound asleep. When

I woke up the next morning, I realized I had overslept, and Leander had left without me. I quickly opened the teepee flap and saw him walking toward his farm with his gray shirttail hanging out.

About five hours later, I was in the field across the road from Leander's farm, cutting grain with a binder. Suddenly, I heard someone screaming my name. Leander's brother David yelled in my direction.

"Stop working. We think Leander drowned!"

I jumped down from the binder and didn't tie the horses or anything. I ran. My mind blanked with shock and disbelief, as my feet pounded the familiar ground to the pond where we had camped the night before. I stood on the bank of the pond, my chest heaving to catch my breath as I stared at the water. *Leander could be in that deep dark pit.*

Leander's clothes were on the bank, but he was nowhere around. Scuba divers were called in, and Amish neighbors gathered around the shore. Hardly anyone talked as we stared out at the water, searching for any sign of Leander. The scuba divers would surface occasionally, but then go back down and continue their search. To describe what I felt would not be possible. Time stood still but lasted forever. I desperately hoped against all odds that somehow Leander would just show up from nowhere and surprise all of us. He was too young to die, and was by far our best swimmer. Hours went by and still no sign of him or his body.

Suddenly, one of the scuba divers poked his head out of the water and nodded. Immediately, we all knew what that meant. They'd found his body. I couldn't believe it, but I had to. It's the most difficult thing I ever experienced my entire life. They pulled his lifeless body from the water, his family identified him, and they zipped him up in a body bag.

At that moment, I thought about the cigarette lighter he

usually carried in his pocket. I broke away from the scene and ran to his house. My feet hammered up the stairs two at a time to his room where I found the lighter. I grabbed it and thrust it into my pocket to protect his secret. My goal was to make sure no one knew he owned a forbidden cigarette lighter. I didn't want someone to think Leander went to hell for disobeying the church rules.

Left alone with my thoughts, I wondered if there was any way we could know Leander was in heaven. I went to one of the preachers in the church and asked, "Do we have any assurance that Leander is in heaven?" I had to know.

I can still hear that old preacher's words when he said, "Well, the Amish church has always taught that a person is unaccountable for his sins until he joins the church. Since Leander was still one year away from becoming a member, we believe his sins are covered, and he's in heaven."

I remember walking away wondering, *Is he right?*

Leander's accident left us wondering what could have happened on that fateful day in 1984. According to his dad, he had been raking hay in a field near the pond. We could only guess that he wanted to let the horses rest, and he took a quick dip to cool off. Since the two-by-twelve diving board was missing from the structure and floating in the water, we had to believe that while he was bouncing and preparing for a dive, the nails pulled out on the back end of the board. Most likely, Leander fell straight down into the water. When his head surfaced, the board somehow flipped end over end, hit his head, and knocked him out. Looking back, I've often wondered why we only used nails.

For many years after Leander's death, I'd regularly dream about him. At times, I blamed myself for being the cause of the accident. To this day I still think of how close we were, and how devastating it was to lose my best friend.

I have always believed, and still do, that God never wastes pain. In Leander's case, God used death to start me on the path to find out if we could have assurance of salvation. I never thought the Bible held the answer, because we were taught to believe what the church believed. But the Bible does have the answer.

> *And this is the record, that **God hath given to us eternal life**, and this life is in his Son. **He that hath the Son hath life**; and he that hath not the Son of God hath not life. These things have I written unto you that believe on the name of the Son of God; **that ye may know that ye have eternal life.***
> (1 John 5:11-13a, emphasis added)

Chapter 9

Life out of Control

By the age of seventeen, I had left the Amish several times, so most parents in the Ashland community had grown leery of my rebellious streaks. They didn't want their children around me, fearing I would get them in trouble, or worse yet, lead them astray. It was then that Levi Miller showed up in my life. He was the Bishop's son and had never left the Amish, but radios, smoking, and alcohol were a big part of his weekends. We quickly became close friends and started hanging out every weekend. On many occasions, we got in our buggy and drove outside of the Amish community where no one could see what we were doing.

We found a place that would sell us alcohol, even though we weren't of age, and most Sundays we'd get drunk. I lived any way I wanted in spite of being a member of the church. At home, I'd get caught having too much to drink, owning a radio, or having cassette tapes, which Dad often smashed with a sledge hammer.

In addition to buying alcohol, we smoked; sometimes I cared, sometimes I didn't. The church publicly disciplined me on numerous occasions. People really cared about me, but I didn't care about people. I was cold and detached from them. I was so into myself it was unbelievable.

What caused me to go down this road? That's a good question. In my mind, much of it goes back to my perception of Dad not having time for me. I so badly wanted his time and approval. When I didn't get it, I gave up and went searching for other ways to fill that void in my life. But I also know *that all things work together for good to them that love God, to them who are the called according to his purpose* (Romans 8:28). God is in control. This verse doesn't say all things are good, but they work together for good, and that is how God ended up working in my life even through these dark times.

Throughout my various escapades, I stole a lot of money from Dad. What a bleak time in my life! And I didn't just steal from Dad. While I was outside the Amish, I went around the Amish community and stole money while they were in church. Later, when I was eighteen, the Lord saved me, and I went and paid all those people back. Some said, "It's not necessary, Joe," but I laid the money in their milk houses.

I even worked for my dad for free to pay him back – not just for the money I stole, but also for the pickup truck I ran into. Dad had covered those bills but asked me to pay him back. When working hours were over for the day, I made wind chimes and sold them for extra money. I hadn't realized Dad knew I'd taken any money. I thought I had been so sly, but just like he knew where I was and what I was doing, he knew I'd been stealing from him.

"I've watched you steal from me over the years," he said. He tallied it to be a thousand dollars.

Amish Dating

When I was struggling through my nine weeks of baptismal

classes, a man in our community tried hard to get me to date his sister-in-law, Esther Yoder. I barely knew her, but I knew of her family. We lived in the same community but on opposite sides. Her house was an hour away by buggy. The motive of this Amish guy trying to set this up was that he was sure if he could hook me up with Esther, I would settle down and stay Amish. The thing is, in my heart, I really didn't want an Amish girlfriend, but I agreed to have one date.

I have to say she wasn't what I expected. Not only was she beautiful and about my height, but I loved the way she talked. As our dating time was winding down for the night, Esther leaned over and left a hickey on the side of my neck. I was slightly embarrassed and glad the kerosene lamp was turned down low enough, so she couldn't see my red face. Since I had never been kissed by a girl before, I tensed up and didn't know how to react. She accepted me just the way I was, and I went home knowing there was something special about this girl that I really liked.

Before I go on with the account of my dating life, I must explain Amish dating to my non-Amish readers. Of course, it varies from one community to the next, but in my community rumspringa (dating) started at age seventeen. What it amounts to is that we held church on Sunday, ate a lunch of pickles, red beets, and bread with a choice of apple butter and homemade peanut butter as a spread, and then all the people went home. On Sunday night, the young people returned to the house where the church service had been held. All the church benches were still set up.

We gathered in the kitchen where the boys and girls faced each other while sitting on the same wooden benches we sat on just a few hours earlier. How many young people gather depends on the size of the community, but generally we had three to four rows of boys and the same for girls. We'd sit there from 8:00

to 10:00 p.m. singing and looking at each other. While still in German, the songs were faster and more up-tempo than those sung during the church service.

The blend of young people includes some guys and girls who are in a dating relationship. Others aren't going steady yet. Until a girl is going steady, all the free guys can try to date her. Girls don't actively pursue the guys, but the guys chase after the girls. The girl can either accept or reject the offer.

The offer itself is often made in a roundabout way. Normally, if I wanted to date a girl like Esther, I wouldn't go to her directly. Instead, I would write her a letter, asking if she would allow me to have a date with her. This process could take up to several weeks and was not a very handy or popular way of scheduling a date. The better way was to send a trustworthy friend to go to her after the singing and ask, "Can Joe Keim take you home tonight?"

If she said no, that was the end of it. If she accepted, you didn't want to let anyone know, which I will explain.

In my case, I sent my trusted friend, Levi Miller, to ask Esther, and she said yes. So he took Esther a mile or two up the road, and then I came along on my buggy and took her the rest of the way home. When I arrived at her house, she climbed out of the buggy while I went out to the barn and put my horse up, because I'd be there until two in the morning.

By the time I put the horse up, Esther had changed into a dating nightgown. I took my hat off and made myself at home. By church standards we could date two different ways. The first involved two chairs facing each other, or some girls like the rocking chair scenario. For the rocking chair, there was only one chair. The guy sat in the chair and girl sat on his lap. I had one experience with this when dating another girl, and my legs grew totally numb. When she got up, I couldn't even get up. I had to let the blood flow back into my legs first.

With Esther, we didn't choose the rocker or the chairs. Instead, we sat on the couch, and often broke the rules and laid on the couch with the warm flicker of the kerosene lamp dancing across us in the small living room. Her parents were in their bedroom right on the other side of the nearby double doors. About halfway through our date, Esther got up and brought in a snack prepared for the two of us. But at 2:00 a.m. time was up and the date over. A couple of times I stayed until 2:30, and her mother banged on the door.

"Time to go."

That's all she said, and I knew I needed to leave.

In Esther's case, at least six other guys courted her. Most of the time I couldn't ask her for a date on a Sunday night, because she was booked up for four to six weeks; and because of the way we did it, I never knew for sure which other guys were seeing her, or if I'd be the guy who ended up going steady with her. For me, it made the situation very hard. On top of that, I found out my trusted friend Levi was also dating Esther, and he never told me! When I found out, I was really hurt.

All of this happened before a boy and girl started going steady. The reason for the secrecy is that you didn't want the other single guys to know you had a date, because they'd sneak around to the houses where they thought a guy might be having his first, second, or third date and play tricks.

One night as Esther and I were having our date, a whole bunch of guys snuck up to Esther's house and pounded on the window. Boy, did that startle us! We couldn't see a thing in the dark so we didn't know who they were; but somehow they knew it was me having a date that night. Sometimes, they took the wheel off the buggy, stuck the axle through the fence, and put the wheel back on, so when the person drove away it would take part of the fence with him. Other times, they'd place trip ropes across the walkway so you'd trip as you were leaving.

Some tricks were pretty nasty. The worst trick played on me happened one night when my horse was nowhere to be found when it came time to leave. The pranksters left the buggy, and I had no idea what had happened to my horse. I didn't know if he'd gotten loose or someone took him. As it turned out, they'd taken my horse up the road to another Amish neighbor's barn, and I didn't get home until time for chores the next morning.

After some time, Esther weeded out her suitors. We had about six dates over eight months, and I fell so in love that I didn't think I could go through life without her. One night these feelings were very heavy on me.

"Tonight you have to tell me if I'm the right guy or not. I can't continue like this – not knowing."

Fear shredded my insides because I worried she'd say no. We talked and talked that night, but she didn't give me an answer. I figured she just couldn't tell me the answer was "no."

I went home unsure of what to think. My world turned upside down days later when I heard Esther had left the Amish. To make matters worse, I learned she'd moved in with some English guy I didn't trust at all. I called an English taxi driver and asked, "Will you take me to see Esther Yoder?"

When I found her, she confided in me. She wasn't happy. The guy she was staying with was married and coming on to her. This planted a new idea in my mind. I begged her to leave the Amish with me.

"The two of us can hang out together, move into town, and get jobs."

She agreed, but in the meantime, she came back to the Amish.

The two of us didn't leave right away, but we made a plan to leave the Amish together and move into town. The following week I picked her up on Sunday evening. We didn't go to the singing but went on a halfway date. We drove out into the neighborhood in the dark and spent our time drinking.

The horse I owned was spirited and tended to be a bit wild and almost uncontrollable at times, particularly at stop signs. Around midnight, we were moving at a pretty good clip. In front of us, an English driver drove right out into the highway. Our buggy slammed into his car. The horse broke free from the buggy, but no one was hurt.

We dragged the buggy over to Esther's house. What a sorry sight we were: drunk and involved in an accident. Her dad caught us dragging my buggy back to her house. He blew up.

"I don't want you dating my daughter. I don't want you ever to come on the property."

I got the full blame that night and deserved it.

Later, just before we were ready to leave the Amish together, the English driver who pulled out in front of my buggy came to my dad's shop and wanted to know how much cash was needed to pay for the damage to my buggy. My heart beat a little faster. This would provide the money we needed to live until we found jobs.

"A thousand dollars would cover the damage," I replied.

The English guy looked at me and said, "That sounds fair enough, and far cheaper than fixing a car."

The deal was made, but as the conversation continued, the deacon of the church walked up and started listening in. Before long he realized what was going on and butted in on the conversation.

"Don't worry about it; we'll take care of it."

The chance to make some easy money walked out the door. At the time, it really irritated me.

Chapter 10

The Gift of Eternal Life

Getting Settled

Within the Amish community, many teens pull away from their parents and get in trouble with the church for things such as having a radio or drinking. In Esther's case, the church constantly harassed her for her dress or head covering being too fancy, and she had her own inner struggles with Amish rules that stemmed back to when she was a young girl. One time, her father told her to go call the veterinarian, but she couldn't understand why it was okay to use the neighbor's phone when they weren't allowed to own one. It seemed to be a double standard. The second time her father asked her to make a call, she cried because she didn't want to use the phone when it was a sin to own one.

"Just go along and do it," her dad said. "This is the way the Amish do it."

These things really bothered her. *If we do the things we do only because that's how we've always done it, I don't want any part of it*, she thought. As children, we were programed to believe certain ways without question. But as we got older, we had to own those beliefs. Most of the time it worked out, and those same beliefs continued to get passed on to the next generation. In my case, I thought it to be rebellion – my disconnect with my father. But really my rebellion could be traced back to the same problem that Esther had. I struggled with these things controlling my life when they didn't make sense.

I was eighteen years old when Esther and I moved into town. We left together and both got our driver's licenses and jobs. She worked for an older lady whom she cared for. I, on the other hand, applied for a local welding job. When they called me in for an interview, I called one of my dad's English customers and asked if he would allow me to come and practice electric welding. I had never welded with an electric welder and wanted to make sure I could do it.

The customer agreed. "Sure, come on out and practice as much as you want."

After several hours of practice, I felt comfortable. The interview and welding test went well, and I got the job making $3.35 an hour, which was minimum wage at the time. I will never forget how great it felt to cash that first week's check.

At first we stayed with someone, but eventually moved into our own apartment. We pretty much lived any way we wanted. My dad constantly came into the welding shop where I worked to remind me I was living with my girlfriend and that sex outside of marriage was wrong. "You'll go to hell," he reminded me.

I didn't see his reaching out like this as a display of love because he cared about what would happen to me. I considered him to be meddlesome and judging. I justified my behavior and lifestyle by letting him know that at least I wasn't going from one woman to another.

I also did what so many others do when they leave the Amish – I threw all the rules out the back door. And since I knew so little about the Bible, I often wasn't sure if the rules were generated by the Amish or if they were actually biblical.

Salvation

God had another plan to reach me. A former Amish family from my community moved in to the apartment next to ours. Paul and his wife, Miriam, had been saved a few years earlier through a Bible study with English people. Because of their openness and evangelism to other Amish families in my community, Paul's concerned parents had come from Wisconsin to try to talk their son and wife out of going to the Bible studies. They were afraid Paul and Miriam would leave the Amish. One January night, while their parents were in the house, Paul, Miriam, and their tiny daughter escaped by crawling out a second-story window and down a ladder. They left their house, property, belongings, and farm animals behind and fled to Kentucky, where they lived for about a year.

When they heard, however, that Esther and I had left the Amish, Paul and Miriam decided to move back to Ohio, and they became our neighbors. They lived right next door to our apartment. Paul tried his best to share the gospel with me, but I didn't want anything to do with it. I figured I had to obey my parents and return to the Amish if I wanted to go to heaven.

From my perspective, Paul and his family seemed to be constantly going to church or some preacher's conference. They attended a mid-sized Baptist church about fifteen minutes out of town. Paul would come home from church all fired up about Jesus. He continually reminded us that we needed to get saved and that the church was praying for us. Much of what he shared did not agree with what Esther and I had been taught growing up; therefore, we blocked most of it out. Besides, I wanted as little to do with church as possible. As far as I was concerned,

Esther and I would never let another church corner us and put us in a box where we didn't fit.

Whenever my dad came to visit us, he'd voice his concern about Paul and Miriam.

"Be very cautious with Paul, because he and Miriam have a strange belief."

I'd agree with Dad and say there's no such thing as getting saved on the spot and having assurance of heaven before we die. Not only did it seem prideful to believe in assurance of salvation, but from Paul's conversations, it sounded like a saved person could live his life any way he wanted and still be accepted by God. Surely he was wrong!

As time went on, Paul brought his pastor to see me. Pastor John Bouquet was a single young man who had just taken over Bethel Baptist Church as senior pastor. He was about my height and had enough energy to move a train. On one occasion, Pastor John invited me to sit in his car. He opened his Bible and began to share how man was not able to save himself from his own sin. Going to church and becoming a member would not take our sin away. Being Amish wouldn't save us from our sins. Being baptized wouldn't do it. Therefore, Jesus Christ, God's only Son, was sent to our planet to die on the cross. It was through His sacrifice – death, burial, and resurrection – that we could have our sins washed away and receive everlasting life.

The pastor went on to say there was only one way to heaven, and it wasn't the Baptist way, nor was it the Amish or Catholic way. It was the Jesus way. He further explained that in John 14:6, the Bible says: *Jesus saith unto him, I am the way, the truth, and the life: no man cometh unto the Father, but by me.* Jesus didn't say "I am a way, a truth, and a life." He claimed to be the way, the truth, and the life. Jesus left no room for other means of salvation. John 10:1 says: *He that entereth not by the door into the sheepfold, but climbeth up some other way, the same is a thief and a robber.*

My guard was up. I refused to allow Paul's or the pastor's words to sink in. In my mind, I had grown up Amish, and in order to be right with God, I had to go back to the Amish, clean my life up, start obeying my parents, and submit to the church rules our forefathers had established. There was no other way.

At my workplace, my boss also witnessed to me. I soon learned his church believed you had to believe in Jesus *plus* get baptized and belong to his denomination in order to be saved. Suddenly, confusion set in, and I began to evaluate all the different beliefs in the world. One church said Jesus alone can save us. Another said you have to believe in Jesus, get baptized, and join their denomination. Back home, they believed I had to obey my parents, get baptized, join the Amish church, follow the ordinance letter, and separate myself from the outside world.

For several weeks, I pondered all the things I was learning about God. But why was it that my boss, the Baptist pastor, and the Amish all read from the same Bible but walked away with different interpretations? One day it came to me how my boss and the Amish both pointed to their church as a means of salvation. They hadn't eliminated Jesus and His sacrifice on the cross, but both parties believed their denomination was God's favorite, and somehow, unless a person became a member of their church, he couldn't be saved. On the other hand, Paul and the Baptist pastor hardly ever mentioned their denomination. They just kept pointing me to Jesus Christ.

While I tried to sort through all the confusion in my mind, I remembered a sermon I once heard while Amish.

The minister said, "It's like this! The people of the world are all making their way toward God on different sides of the mountain. When we get to the top, God will sort it all out." He went on to say, "According to Ephesians 6:2, God's first commandment to children everywhere is to obey their parents. If your parents are Amish, obey and follow their teachings. If you were born and raised in some other religious system, obey and follow their teachings."

And then the preacher concluded by giving out the ever famous quote: "Bloom where God planted you and you will be in the center of His will."

One hot July Sunday afternoon Paul said, "I need a little time with you away from all the noise."

He had just come home from church and was all fired up and determined to talk to me about Jesus. I hesitated, but agreed and got in his car. I remember the day well. It was July 28, 1985.

Paul took me through town and out in the country. Finally, he slowed down and turned into a driveway. We got out of the car and slowly walked to a grassy spot and sat down. Paul pulled his Bible out and explained that the book of Romans tells a person how to get saved from sin and hell. He opened to Romans and began reading.

Paul said, "Every single person on the face of the earth stands before God a sinner. It makes no difference if the person grew up in a Christian home, has gone to church all his life, gotten baptized, or is in full-time ministry. The Bible says: *There is none righteous, no, not one* (Romans 3:10)."

"I know I'm a sinner," I admitted with a shrug.

However, in my mind there were bad sinners and good sinners. And since I had never committed a crime so bad it landed me in prison, I considered myself on the side of the good sinners. Then I went on to tell him about my Uncle Albert.

"He was a deacon in the Amish church. If anyone will go to heaven, it is Uncle Albert." He was the most honest man I ever met. He was kindhearted and caring. He served the church with much compassion and often cried when people were hurting.

"Surely," I said, "if anyone in the world is going to heaven, it's Uncle Albert."

Paul quickly responded, "In Romans 3:23, the Bible says, *For all have sinned and come short of the glory of God,* even Uncle Albert."

At that moment, I felt heavy scales lifting away from the eyes of my heart. It was so real! For the first time in my life, I understood sin as described in the Bible. In a moment, I realized there was no such thing as good sinners and bad sinners.

Paul continued. "In another part of the Bible, it says, *Whosoever shall keep the whole law, and yet offend in one point, he is guilty of all* (James 2:10)."

This helped me understand that it's not a matter of doing the best we can or doing better than someone else. It's all or nothing. We have to be perfect, because breaking the slightest commandment is like breaking them all. If we never steal, kill, or commit adultery but fail to love God with all our hearts, souls, and strength, we are just as guilty as the murderer.

That day, the Holy Spirit taught me that I fall short. There's no way possible for me to be good enough to go to heaven. *For the wages of sin is death; but the gift of God is eternal life through Jesus Christ our Lord* (Romans 6:23). The gift of God is eternal life through Jesus Christ, not through the Amish church, not by being baptized at seventeen or because I did something special, but because of Jesus Christ. *For by grace are ye saved through faith; and that not of yourselves: it is the gift of God: Not of works, lest any man should boast* (Ephesians 2:8-9). Paul said salvation is not of works; it isn't something you work for, but it is a gift from God. Like any gift, it has to be received, and *whosoever shall call upon the name of the Lord shall be saved* (Romans 10:13).

When Paul asked if I would like to call on the Lord for salvation, I couldn't help but say yes. I was utterly convicted of my sins and realized there was only one way out of my mess and that was to fully trust in Jesus Christ and what He did for me on the cross. As we bowed our heads before God and began to pray, the Holy Spirit came upon me. It was as if God opened the doors of heaven and poured out an immeasurable amount of love on me. I felt all my sins being washed away. It was so real! I cried and cried. The love of God entered my heart. I had no doubt but that I had an encounter with the living God.

Later in life, after I began to study the Bible, I realized even more what had taken place that day in July of 1985. When one is born into God's family, many things happen instantly:

- The believer is instantly reconciled to God, becomes a new creation, and is forgiven for all his sins (2 Corinthians 5:17-19).

- The believer is delivered from the power of darkness (Colossians 1:13).

- The believer is sealed with the Holy Spirit (Ephesians 1:13; 4:30).

- The believer is perfected forever (Hebrews 10:14).

- The believer has eternal life and shall never perish (John 10:28).

Jesus said, *He that heareth my word, and believeth on him that sent me, HATH everlasting life, and SHALL NOT come into condemnation; but is PASSED from death unto life* (John 5:24, emphasis added). Everlasting life is not a future experience that takes place after we die (John 3:36; 6:47). Jesus said those who believe on Him have everlasting life now. John 17:3 defines everlasting life as knowing the only true God and Jesus Christ. This is talking about intimacy with God, and that is everlasting life.

I went back to the apartment and told Esther.

"I can't fully explain what all took place today, but I know I got saved."

At first, she seemed almost angry that I had fallen for Paul's strange beliefs. After several arguments and much persistence on my part, Esther agreed she would visit the Baptist church with me.

The next Sunday we went, and it just so happened that the pastor preached on salvation. My girlfriend was sitting straight up in her pew and taking every word to heart. She remembered reading some storybooks that introduced her to the message of salvation, and she always wondered about it. When she was in the fifth grade, the Gideons showed up at her one-room schoolhouse and handed her an English New Testament, which she often read and tried to understand. At a young age, the Holy Spirit had already begun a work in her heart preparing her for this day.

When the sermon came to an end, the pastor extended an invitation to anyone searching for God and wanting to be saved. By now, tears painted wet streaks on Esther's cheeks. She wanted to know how she, too, could be born again. Slowly she left her seat and moved into the aisle to walk forward to the altar. One of the older ladies took her into the back room and explained the gospel. She heard the same good news, believed it with her whole heart, and was saved.

Now that Esther and I were born again, the Holy Spirit convicted us about living together before marriage. The thought of separating seemed unbearable. To get married in the English culture wasn't something I wanted to do, because truthfully, I had always dreamed of having an Amish wedding.

Several weeks later, Dad came to visit me.

"Joe, I'm going to give you a choice. If you come back to the Amish within the next two weeks, I'll take you back, but if you don't, I'll cut you off. You can't come back on the property. You can't see any other family, either."

That really hit me hard. I couldn't imagine never going back, never seeing the rest of my family. Esther didn't want to follow me back to the Amish, but I said, "Promise me that if I go back and stay a month, you will follow me."

Reluctantly, she promised. I sold my car and returned home.

Chapter 11

Shunning

Soon after I came back, the deacon of the church pressured me to go to town with him and destroy all worldly evidence that was still connected to me. First, we drove to the place where I had gotten my driver's license a few months earlier. When we arrived, the two of us got out of our buggy and walked inside to get in line to talk with one of the ladies behind the counter.

As always, the line was long and customers looked at us as if we were from another planet. But there we were, all dressed in Amish garb, standing out like sore thumbs. I'm sure everybody wondered what in the world two Amish men were doing at the driver's license bureau.

We finally made it all the way to the front of the line.

"We are here today because of Joe and his driver's license. I'd like for you to go into your system and destroy all evidence of his records," the deacon said.

To say I was embarrassed is an understatement, but my parents and the church leaders felt my identity with the world must become nonexistent, and they didn't want me carrying a photo ID around in my pocket for fear it would break the second commandment, Exodus 20:4: *Thou shalt not make unto thee any graven image, or any likeness of anything that is in heaven above, or that is in the earth beneath, or that is in the water under the earth.*

The ladies at the license bureau had never done anything like this before, so they grouped together and discussed the situation in whispering tones. We could hear them giggling and glancing back at us. I wanted to die. Why did I ever go back to the Amish? Finally, they came back and said all trace of my identity had been wiped from their system.

"If you ever change your mind about driving a car, you'll have to retake the driving test and apply for another license."

From the license bureau, we went to the music store where Esther had bought me a fiddle for Christmas. I loved musical instruments and wanted so badly to learn how to play the fiddle. For several months, I had taken music lessons and I was doing quite well on the strings. But now that I was Amish again, the fiddle had to go. The guy at the music store said, "No problem, we can sell it for you," and we left it.

A few weeks later, I called Esther and asked if she would go back to the store and get the fiddle again, and she did. She brought it to me, and I hid it underneath my bed.

An old saying, "A man convinced against his will is of the same opinion still," contains a lot of truth. What I found with myself and others in the Amish community was that many times because of the stringent church rules, we lived double lives. On numerous occasions, a young person left the community because of the weight and guilt that came with living a double life.

John, a member of the Old Order Amish church, once told me the true story of how he carried a forbidden cell phone in his pocket. He worked alongside his older brother Amos, who followed and lived the Amish law to a tee. Amos was known to turn anybody in to the church deacon for breaking a church rule. One time when John's cell phone started vibrating in his pocket, he quickly left the building, went out the back door, and crawled through the long weeds on hands and knees. John kept going deeper and deeper into the weeds to make sure Amos would not see or hear him respond to the phone call.

Finally, he felt safe. But as he reached into his pocket for the phone, he heard someone else talking just a few feet away. It was his brother Amos, also hiding in the weeds and calling someone from his own phone.

Jesus had this to say about hypocrisy:

> *Woe unto you, scribes and Pharisees, hypocrites!*
> *for ye are like unto whited sepulchres, which indeed*
> *appear beautiful outward, but are within full of*
> *dead men's bones, and of all uncleanness. Even*
> *so ye also outwardly appear righteous unto men,*
> *but within ye are full of hypocrisy and iniquity.*
> (Matthew 23:27-28)

Because I was a member of the church, I was shunned for a season, at least until my hair grew back from really short to over my ears. This would take about two months. During this time, I couldn't eat with my family and had to sit at a separate table by myself. Church was the same; everyone observed my shame. It was very humiliating.

I had given up everything to come back, and still they shunned me. One day while I worked in my dad's machine shop, a man from the community asked me for something in my hand. I extended my hand to give it to him, but he wouldn't take it. "I can't take it from your hand," he said. That guy purposely humiliated me on top of all I was going through. I had to lay it down; then he picked it up.

Esther came back and joined the Amish about a month

later. The church forbade us to see each other, so I'd sneak out my window at night and ride bareback to Esther's place. She'd sneak out, and we'd meet at her dad's leather shop. Since we didn't have phones or any other way to connect, I'd ride out there about every other night. One time we were caught, and the church extended the shunning another two weeks. This shunning and these sanctimonious rules wore on Esther and me.

One day, Paul, the one who led me to the Lord, sent me a note saying they were going to a Billy Graham crusade in Washington, DC. While there, they planned see the White House. He wrote, "You and Esther are invited to go with us if you want. It won't cost you anything."

I couldn't turn Paul's offer down. Esther and I were highly frustrated with the Amish church and the way members were treating us. We both agreed we would go with Paul and his family.

I went to bed that night, and after Ervin drifted off to sleep, I opened the side window, shimmied down a rope to a tree, and dropped to the ground. Paul was waiting on the road and picked me up first. Then we drove to Esther's house and picked her up. After that, we headed straight to Washington, DC. I remember very few details about this trip, except that I was overjoyed to be with my girlfriend again. I felt restored and invigorated when free from all those people who continued to humiliate us by shunning us openly and publicly.

After being away for three days, I arrived home to find that things were different. My family had gone through all my belongings and divided them up among themselves. This included everything, even my guns. Some of it I never got back. From my family's point of view, this was the fifth time I'd run away, even though I was only gone for a couple of days.

Esther and I got fed up with the ongoing humiliation of shunning. Couldn't the Amish church see that we had given up everything to come back? We had sold our cars and given up our jobs. That meant no more income for us; instead, we worked for our parents for free. During all of this, the church refused to let us see each other. Weeks turned into months. Depression set in and life was almost not worth living. It was so hard!

Then I remembered an old English friend by the name of Chuck, who had said, "If you ever decide to leave the Amish, you can live with me." He lived in Mount Vernon, Ohio, which was about an hour away by car.

I found Chuck's phone number, and I called to explain our situation.

"Sure, you can come and live with my wife and me and my family," he said. "I'll give you a job trimming cow hooves."

So we set a date for a Sunday night. I traveled out to Esther's place and left my horse and buggy in her father's barn. Esther and I walked about a mile up the road and sat in the ditch in the weeds, waiting for Chuck to come pick us up in his truck. Crickets chirped and mosquitoes hummed as the sun set. Dampness set in as we waited in complete darkness. No one knew about our plans except Chuck, who was picking us up in a short while.

What I didn't know was that my dad had followed me out to Esther's place. He sat in the opposite ditch, knowing something was up. Headlights sliced through the pitch dark, and we darted from the ditch so Chuck would see us and stop. At that moment, my dad jumped out of the ditch and started yelling my name, crying bitterly, and begging me to stay. It scared us, but we quickly jumped on the back of the truck bed. Chuck sped off into the night.

My dad quickly disappeared into the darkness and dust. To this day, when I think back to that moment, my heart breaks for my dad. He may not have been the perfect father, but it was so unfair that he had to once again deal with my escape from the

Amish. I can't imagine what he went through at that moment, but my dad never gave up.

After we lived with Chuck for a month, my dad got a feeling things weren't going to work out between us and Chuck. So, unbeknown to me, he went to the Mount Vernon police and told them what to do if I showed up looking for help.

I rode to work with Chuck. The work was fine, but many times on the way home, he stopped at gentlemen's clubs while I waited in the car. Then he tried to proposition Esther, which bothered her so much that she went back to the Amish. This annoyed me too, and I also decided to go back to the Amish. I went to Chuck to let him know, and his temper flared.

"Get out of the house or I'll kill you!" he yelled. "Never come back!"

He didn't even let me get my things.

I ran from the house in the middle of the night bawling. I didn't know where to turn for help, and the only thing I knew to do was find the police station. When I did, they said, "We were prepared for this. Your dad already talked to us."

They called an Amish taxi driver to pick me up and take me back to my parents. It was quite an ordeal, and the consequences added several months of shunning. Eventually, the church couldn't find any more faults, and they took us back into fellowship. What a wonderful relief that was for us and for the church too. For the first time in about a year, life was back to normal.

Chapter 12

Marriage

With the shunning period complete, Esther and I were allowed to see each other on a weekly basis. We'd go to the singing and have a date on Sunday night just like normal. Several months passed by and marriage became a hot subject between Esther and me. We had been through so much together and couldn't imagine not getting married and living life together.

First, we went to our parents and got their permission. They seemed excited and supported our decision wholeheartedly. After that, it was customary to go to Esther's bishop and get his permission also. We waited until dark, so no one could see us traveling together in the same buggy during a weekday. At first, the bishop was a bit hesitant because Esther, even though a member of the church, had never participated in a communion service. Finally, after some pleading on our part, he agreed.

"Under your circumstances, I am going to make an exception and give you permission to get married."

A couple of things are unique about Amish weddings. First, weddings always take place on Tuesdays or Thursdays, mostly Thursdays. Secondly, until the Bishop announces your wedding, it stays a secret. Only your immediate family and the Bishop know in advance. You don't want anyone in the community to know, because it's supposed to be a surprise. The person who announces the happy news is the Bishop from the girl's district.

I got up early on Sunday morning and headed toward Esther's church district. On this day Bishop Dan would announce our wedding day to the whole church. As Mike pulled my buggy along State Route 603, my heart was beating twice as fast as normal. For the first time in my life, I felt as though things were coming together for me. Soon, Esther Yoder would change her last name to Keim and become my dearly beloved wife. The thought was so precious, I could hardly contain it all. As I drove in the lane where church services were being held that day, I thought, *Only the Bishop and Esther's parents know about the big announcement.*

I had barely finished unhitching Mike before someone walked by and yelled, "We know why you are here today."

Oh no, I thought. *Someone let the cat out of the bag.* But to my surprise, no one else said a word.

The church service moved along very slowly as each minister got up and did his part. Everyone was half asleep except for me. I was wide awake. Finally, the last minister finished and sat down.

Next, Bishop Dan got up, cleared his throat, and said, "Today I have a surprise announcement to make. Joe Keim and Esther Yoder have been granted permission to get married and have set their wedding date for December 18. You are all invited."

As soon as the Bishop announced our plans, Esther and I walked out, in proper Amish fashion, before the service ended. I ran out to hitch up the horse and buggy, and we were on our way before people were released from the church service.

The next two weeks were a whirlwind of activity at Esther's home place, as we prepared for the wedding. We mailed out invitations, hauled all the manure out of the barn, rearranged the house furniture, brought wedding tables down from the attic, and set them up. Family members stopped in about every day to help prepare the food, make the multilevel wedding cake, and help decorate the corner where the wedding party would sit to eat.

One evening, after I came home from Esther's place, Dad said, "I don't want any of your English friends at the wedding."

"Dad, I already invited Larry Holbrook to the wedding."

"Well," he replied, "I guess you'll have to tell him different."

I couldn't believe Dad was going to make me uninvite Larry, just because he was English. I was almost twenty years old – old enough to make my own decisions. Besides that, I felt it was my wedding. Larry and I discussed the situation and decided if he wore Amish clothes, it would all work out. Nothing more was said to Dad about Larry coming to the wedding.

After many hours and little sleep, the big day arrived. December 18, 1986, was a cold day, but hardly any snow covered the ground. By 9:00 a.m. hundreds of family members and friends from several states away had gathered together under one roof to help us celebrate our special day. The three-hour ceremony took place at a neighbor's house, right across the field from Esther's home place.

My friend Larry showed up wearing Amish clothes; he fit right in with the rest of the people at the wedding. No one, except my own family, knew he wasn't Amish. Before long though, Dad spotted Larry and became very upset – so upset that he left right after the ceremony and went home.

While wedding attenders sat on regular wooden church benches without backs, the wedding party sat on two rows of chairs – in the center of the living room – three girls facing three guys. We sat with two unmarried couples; two girls sat on either side of Esther, and two guys sat on either side of me. They were the witnesses who followed us throughout the day, always sitting on either side of us.

Soon after the singing began, all the preachers got up and left the room to have their traditional meeting behind closed doors. Several minutes went by, and then Esther and I got up from our chairs and followed their path to a room upstairs. As we sat there in a circle, I was reminded of my baptismal classes, only this time I was there because I chose to be there. I cannot recall a word that was said in that setting, except the ministers warned us that we could not have sex until the third day. I just remember thinking, *You've gotta be kidding me! Three days! Whoever came up with that one?*

Now that our meeting with the preachers was over and we were once again sitting in our chairs between our four witnesses, the preaching began. Just like regular church services, most of the ceremony, including the vows, was spoken in High German and difficult to follow. My Uncle Joe, whom I was named after, was my favorite community bishop, and he was the one who married us. While we sat waiting for him to call us forward, he talked about biblical weddings, starting with Adam and Eve. He took other parts of his sermon from the Apocrypha, a set of books sandwiched between the Old and New Testament.

Finally, near the end of the ceremony, Uncle Joe called Esther and me to come forward and say our vows to each other. This was the moment we had all been waiting for. As we stood to our feet, our witnesses on both sides also stood with us. Esther and I made our way up and stood side by side before Bishop Joe and all the wedding attendees. After saying our vows to each other, the Bishop reminded us that we were now one flesh and only death could separate us.

After the ceremony, Esther and I and our witnesses were taxied over to Esther's house, where the noon and evening dinner took place. Right before we entered the house, someone threw a broom in front of Esther's path. It is said that if the bride picks the broom up and sets it aside, she will be a great housekeeper. If she steps over it, she will end up being a slob. Yep, Esther picked it up.

Married people gathered around the tables and ate first. Esther and I were seated in a corner that had been decorated with flowers, homemade name ornaments, and a big wedding cake. The witnesses sat at the table with us, only this time one couple sat on Esther's side and one couple sat on my side. We were sandwiched between them. Esther wore a brand new dark blue dress cut from the same pattern as all her other dresses. After the wedding, it would become her Sunday dress.

Esther and I and our witnesses had special servers waiting on us all day long. The menu included a big meal of noodles, mashed potatoes and gravy, two or three different types of meat, and date pudding – a specialty served at every wedding. In fact, date pudding was only served at weddings, and everybody loved it.

While we ate with all the married couples and their families downstairs, the unmarried men were busy partnering up with a girl upstairs. Of course, the couples who were already in a steady dating relationship did not have to choose a partner. But for those others who didn't have a steady relationship with a girl, this was their time to reach out and invite a girl to sit with them at the table. Not only was this a nerve-racking time for the guys, but the girls also tensed up as they waited and hoped for one of the guys to ask them. While the fellows suffered and the gals tensed up, the old folks downstairs couldn't wait to see who would partner up with whom.

When everyone finished eating round one, they quickly cleared the tables, and the Bishop called on the single adults to come downstairs with their partners by their side and have a seat. This was round two for us and the four witnesses. First, we ate with the married people, now we would eat again with the unmarried adults. As we ate, the married men gathered in the background and sang wedding hymns – some from the hymnbook used in church and some from the hymnbooks used for the Sunday night singing. Both were used to celebrate this transitional time.

People attending our wedding had come from all over, including Indiana and other surrounding states. We probably had four hundred people. If this seems like a lot, you have to remember we had big families, and it wasn't uncommon to have two to three hundred first cousins and lots of aunts and uncles. After the wedding, everyone stood around and caught up on what was happening with other family members.

That evening, around seven o'clock, we had another huge meal with immediate family. Dad returned for the latter part of the wedding and joined us for the evening meal. The celebration continued until about midnight, and finally the tired guests left, and the rest of us went to bed. The next day we woke to tons and tons of dishes to wash.

———

Dad had talked to me about working for him free of charge. He felt it would be a form of penance, and God would forgive me for all the times I'd left the Amish. I really did want to settle down, so I was willing to do what Dad wanted me to do, but that resulted in the problem of not having any income. We lived with Esther's parents and ate with them. We lived there for nine months. Every day I'd commute to my dad's machine shop, and even though I was twenty years old, I didn't take any pay.

We lived along a busy highway, which made it possible to make a little money by gathering nightcrawlers to sell. Esther used the nightcrawler money to buy ingredients to make noodles, which she sold for an income, and my father-in-law took care of the expense of feeding my horse. During that time, I determined I'd settle down and I actually began to connect with my dad as we worked together. A few times he didn't like things I was doing, and we butted heads, but for the most part we got along well.

My goal was to stay Amish and raise a family in the Amish culture. I appreciated the sense of security and protection within that community that I hadn't felt in the English world. The thought of having a family and raising my children outside of those protective boundaries also seemed overwhelming. Life was great and moved along for several months. I loved living with Esther's parents and hanging out with her brother Milo at night. We got along just fine and had many heart-to-heart conversations.

Hunger for Truth

One day, during our in-between church Sunday, Esther picked up the Bible and started reading from the book of Romans. "Why do we live Amish when we are saved?" she asked.

My first thought was, *Wow, I hadn't heard the term "being saved" in months.* Along the way, I had forced my mind and attitude to align with the Amish way of thinking and became angry when Esther talked about her understanding of the Bible.

Immediate fear set in because of where this could lead. I made it clear, "Esther, we are not going down that road again. Please!"

But Esther kept reading, and occasionally we would end up in a hefty Bible discussion because of something she read.

Gradually the stress of Esther's Bible views and us not having a lot of money to spend led me to pick up an old habit of dipping snuff. I had promised Esther, before we got married, that I would quit. And I did. It was the only way she would marry me. It didn't help that many of the people in my life also chewed tobacco, including my father-in-law, who was a preacher in the church. The church didn't allow tobacco chewing and always disciplined members publicly, but many still struggled with the habit.

Paul Coblentz, the man who led me to the Lord a few years earlier, invited Esther to join his family at a Bible study that was taking place at the Baptist church where Esther got saved. She went several times, but I refused to join them. We struggled in our marriage relationship even more. Esther was upset because I continued dipping snuff, and I was upset at her going to Bible studies.

One morning, as I was preparing to leave for my dad's shop, she said, "I've had enough! I'm sick of your snuff, and I don't believe the Amish are preaching the truth."

With that, she walked down the lane that led to the woods. I was going to let her go, but after she walked a quarter of a mile, all the way into the woods and almost out of sight, I realized I couldn't let this happen. I ran out after her and lashed out in extreme anger. We both ended up crying and wondered if there was any way to solve our issues.

Esther's heart was no longer with the Amish and their man-made rules. She wanted to be free to go to Bible studies and participate in prayer meetings – prayer meetings where they prayed without a prayer book. She had, at this point, studied the book of Romans quite extensively and was determined that we were out of God's will. The Amish preached some grace, but mostly works. According to the apostle Paul, grace and works do not mix. It's either all grace or all works. *And if by grace, then is it no more of works: otherwise grace is no more grace. But if it be of works, then is it no more grace: otherwise work is no more work* (Romans 11:6).

We had both experienced such freedom in Christ and the true grace of God when we got saved. Now suddenly, Esther, more so than me, felt we had been pulled back into bondage. She was unhappy in her heart and kept referring to God's Word.

> *I marvel that ye are so soon removed from him that called you into the grace of Christ unto another gospel: Which is not another; but there be some that trouble you, and would pervert the gospel of Christ. But though we, or an angel from heaven, preach any other gospel unto you than that which we have preached unto you, let him be accursed. As we said before, so say I now again, If any man preach any other gospel unto you than that ye have received, let him be accursed. For do I now persuade men, or God? or do I seek to please men? for if I yet pleased men, I should not be the servant of Christ.*
> (Galatians 1:6-10)

Pleasing men rather than God and feeling as though we were living in a box made both of us feel trapped and out of God's will. Despite how we both felt, Esther decided to stay Amish for the time being.

Things got a lot better in our marriage. Esther stopped going to Bible studies with Paul. I stopped dipping snuff. I can't say we were happy, but it did feel good to know that we were making our parents and everybody else happy.

One day, my dad asked if I could stay over one evening and help the rest of the family shock wheat. I agreed, if we could arrange for Esther to come with me to work the next day. So Esther went with me to the machine shop and helped Mom while I took care of Dad's customers. Later that night, after we began to shock wheat, I bummed a dip of snuff off one of my brothers. Somehow Esther caught on and immediately anger set into her heart. This led to us getting into a huge argument. It was okay that she smoked, but I couldn't dip snuff. It made no sense to me. Around and around we went.

Finally, she said, "I've had enough. I'm leaving you and the Amish," and she started walking toward the road.

By this time, the sun had gone down and darkness had settled in, but we still had several hours of shocking left. I was very angry at myself. I was angry at Esther. And it seemed as if life was all about pleasing others.

Finally, about midnight, my family and I got to the end of the field. The entire wheat field was now shocked, and I was ready to head home. I had no idea where Esther was, and I tried my best to keep my family from knowing any of the details. As I headed out with Mike and the two-wheeled cart, I wondered if I would ever see her again. The one-hour drive toward home was a mental nightmare. The tears were uncontrollable as I cried out to God from the depth of my heart.

"Lord, please help me make sense of life!" As I thought about giving in to Esther's wish to leave the Amish, I cried even harder. "I can't do this to my dad and mom. They have been through so much with me!"

Suddenly, something caught the left side of my eye. Was that a mailbox or a person I just passed? I drove a little farther and decided to turn Mike and the cart around and do a double check. I got my flashlight out and began to fervently shine it around the area where I saw the dark object on the side of the road. Sure enough, it was Esther. She had walked for miles along the dark country road. After some coaxing on my part, she crawled onto my cart, and we continued our way home.

Esther finally decided it wasn't going to work for her to force me to leave the Amish, so she handed everything over to God and walked away. She had finally concluded that this battle she was in fully belonged to the Lord, not her.

On the very same day she gave up trying to force me to leave and put it in God's hands, I came home from work and said,

"Esther, I feel as if God is calling us to leave the Amish. I feel dead and empty inside."

To this day, Esther loves to share the story of how God took over the moment she let go. It was as if someone flipped a light switch. It was that quick! It was that real for both of us. The truth is, there are times we think we let go of the battle in our lives, but it's not until later that we truly know we let go. As Esther would say, "As long as you have ahold of your battle, God will let you fight it on your own."

What God did for King Jehoshaphat, the tribe of Judah and Samuel, He will do for you and me. *Thus saith the LORD unto you, Be not afraid nor dismayed by reason of this great multitude;* **for the battle is not yours, but God's** (2 Chronicles 20:15b, emphasis added). *And all this assembly shall know that the LORD saveth not with sword and spear:* **for the battle is the LORD'S**, *and he will give you into our hands* (1 Samuel 17:47, emphasis added).

Leaving

We set a date and a time for Paul Coblentz to come with a pickup truck and a horse trailer to pick up our few belongings and move us into town. We planned to leave on a Sunday morning after Esther's parents left for church.

I got up early on Saturday morning, ate a quick breakfast, and headed for the barn to get Mike and my two-wheeled cart ready to make one last trip to my parents' place, where I would give my dad one more day of free labor. As I threw the harness over Mike and hitched him onto my cart, I patted him on the neck.

"Mike, you and I have traveled many miles, but today will be our last run together. After this, you will be traded in for a car."

As Mike and I traveled along the country roads toward my parents' place, my heart was once again overflowing with emotions. I agonized with my thoughts. *Today, I'm dressed in Amish clothes, driving a horse and cart, living in a slower-paced culture. I have free and easy access to my family, childhood friends, and community. Tomorrow, it will all change. Esther and I will lose it all in one day.*

At my dad's machine shop, I looked at all the work that was piled up and wondered who would take over when I left. By this time, Dad had given me the responsibility of running the shop and caring for customers' needs. After my departure, Dad would have to pick up where I left off. I wished it were somehow possible to sit down and discuss these things with him, but under the circumstances, that was not possible. They would have to fumble their way through on their own.

At lunchtime, I shut all the shop machinery down and headed for the house, where our entire family of fifteen, including Dad and Mom, would gather around the table for one last meal together. Only they did not know it was the last. By this time tomorrow, I would be classified as an outsider and a lost soul. To say I was torn up on the inside is an understatement.

Like any other day, mealtime was family catch-up time. It was not uncommon for several family members to be talking and laughing at the same time. But there I sat; I couldn't eat. My mind was in a whirlwind and Mom noticed.

"Joe, what's the matter with you today?"

"Ah, not much. Just feeling a bit under the weather," I said.

In my heart, I knew Mom would recall our last conversation ten thousand times. Once again, I wished I could just sit down and explain everything, but that would be like inviting an entire army of opposition, begging, tears, and broken hearts.

I woke up with a start on Sunday morning. Church services would soon begin across the field from our house – the same place where Esther and I had exchanged our wedding vows just nine months earlier. As we lay in bed, we talked about our daring plans and made last-minute decisions.

"Joe, you're gonna have to let my parents know that we are not attending church today," she urged.

Hesitantly, I crawled out of bed and walked over to my in-law's part of the house and informed them we would not be at the service that morning.

My father-in-law said, "Then I'll stay home too."

That's not going to work, I thought. People were coming at 9:00 to help move. "Okay, I'll go to church," I said.

With that, my father-in-law agreed to go also. It was as if Esther's parents knew something was up, but they never, in the years after that, said anything to us about it. I put on church clothes and took off walking across the field where the others gathered. Esther stayed home to direct our friends in the move.

When I walked into the barn where the men were, my father-in-law recognized me and nodded his head as if to say he was happy with my decision. By 8:40, all the preachers started making their way toward the house. Because Esther's dad was a preacher, he was in the first group to leave the barn. At the moment I saw him enter the house, I turned and fled without saying a word to anyone. I ran out the back door, across the field, and into our house where Paul Coblentz and others were carrying our belongings out to the truck.

They flung pillows and bedding out the upstairs windows to the ground below. Others rushed around, gathered our goods, and loaded the truck. It only took fifteen minutes to load all of our possessions.

Before we left, I wrote a note to my father-in-law and my parents to explain why we were leaving the Amish. I shook uncontrollably and cried bitterly. When I finished, I looked at the note. It didn't make sense, so I tore it up and wrote a second note and then a third. I threw all of them away. With a gripping sorrow in my heart, I knew that anything I wrote wouldn't make sense to those we were leaving behind. I knew the immense hurt and pain I would bring my dad and mom again. I knew this would be the last time I would ever leave the Amish, and I would never return.

This time, I didn't leave out of rebellion, but out of a true desire to grow in my faith. In order for Esther and me to grow in our faith, we had to go to a church where they not only preached the true gospel – by grace alone, faith alone, and Christ alone – but where the preaching and worship were better understood. We both struggled to understand the High German used for sermons in the Amish setting. In the English church, they preached in the language we learned while attending eight years of school.

The passage of Scripture that challenged us as much as any is Luke 14:26-33, where Jesus challenges all believers:

> *If any man come to me, and hate not his father, and mother, and wife, and children, and brethren, and sisters, yea, and his own life also, he cannot be my disciple. And whosoever doth not bear his cross, and come after me, cannot be my disciple. For which of you, intending to build a tower, sitteth not down first, and counteth the cost, whether he have sufficient to finish it? Lest haply, after he hath laid the foundation, and is not able to finish it, all that behold it begin to mock him, Saying, This man began to build, and was not able to finish. Or what king, going to make war against another king, sitteth not down first, and consulteth whether he be able with ten thousand to meet him that cometh against him with twenty thousand? Or else, while the other is yet a great way off, he sendeth an ambassage, and desireth conditions of peace. So likewise, whosoever he be of you that forsaketh not all that he hath, he cannot be my disciple.*

Chapter 13

Getting Started

Our friend Paul Coblentz, who led me to the Lord, went to church with the Gess family. He made connections with them for us, and Esther and I moved in with this family, though we had never met them before. Jerry and Carol Gess immediately accepted us as their children, and opened their attic for us to live in until we found a place of our own. We pulled up with our belongings and carried all the stuff up to the attic. For the Gesses, the attic was a storage area. Stuff littered the steps all the way up. At the top, boxes and other items filled the unfinished space, with a little path cutting through the boxes and leading to a bed – our bed. It was awesome for us – a haven. And for meals, we ate with them.

Jerry and Carol said, "From this day on, you are family," and they meant it. They put forth every effort to make us feel like family, and their children – Randy, Debbie, and Rene' – did too. When Randy passed away from a heart condition, I felt like I'd lost a brother – a real, true, blood brother. As for Debbie and Rene' they were and are very much a part of our family gatherings. They've always included us as if we are family;

our kids know them as grandparents and aunts, and we spend every Thanksgiving and Christmas with them. We have even taken vacations together.

This family connection is so real that when Debbie got cancer, I was one of the first ones she called. We were there for her hospital visits, and over the years, we've all supported one another as we've been in the hospital, always sitting through the waiting times together. As for Debbie's cancer, it is gone. We prayed that God would deliver her from cancer, and He did. Today, she continues to be cancer free. Her sister Rene' serves as my full-time secretary at MAP Ministry. So many times, God's eternal family is closer than blood family.

The Gess family taught us the importance of going to church, Sunday school, and Wednesday and Sunday night services. One thing that impacted us more than anything else – they showed us what unconditional love looks like. Growing up, I thought love and acceptance were based on my ability to measure up. The Gesses kicked that right out from under us. We've seen them reach out and love people unconditionally again and again. Jerry and Carol filled a void in these thirty years and played an important role in our lives. Today, I know them better than I know my own parents.

Our first Christmas with them was overwhelming. We were accustomed to maybe getting a pair of gloves or some other needed item as a gift. That first Christmas with the Gess family was unbelievable! They poured the gifts on us. I'd never had anyone do that.

They helped us get jobs, buy clothes, and get our driver's licenses back. They even taught us how to make sure the clothes we wore matched. It might sound silly, but with so many different clothing patterns and colors to choose from, we didn't know how to dress. This was all part of our transition from Amish to English.

We lived with Jerry and Carol for about a year. Within a month, I landed a welding job, making minimum wage. Since we had saved up $600 from nightcrawler sales, we decided to go looking for a car.

English friends of ours said, "Our neighbor is selling his car, why don't you come look at it?"

When we got there, I realized it was a stick shift. I had never driven a stick shift, but told the owner it wouldn't be a problem at all.

"Go ahead and take it for a spin," he said.

I jumped in the driver's seat of that older Ford Granada, put it in first gear, pulled out of the driveway, and headed up Route 545 toward Olivesburg. Before long, I decided to turn around and head back. I slowed down and pulled into a driveway. At that moment, I realized I didn't know how to put it in reverse. After struggling for ten minutes and trying every which way to get it in reverse, the farmer came out to see what was going on. I described my problem to him and he offered advice.

"All you have to do is pull up on the shifter, which will then allow you to move the shifter into position." He laughed.

I felt dumb, but I decided I wasn't going to explain my situation. I drove back to the owner's place and inquired about the price.

"How much do you want for your car?" I asked, knowing the value of the car was right at $2,000, and I wouldn't be able to afford it.

He said, "I understand you and Esther just left the Amish, so my wife and I would just like to give it to you."

I couldn't believe what I was hearing. This man didn't even know me. How could he just hand the keys to his car over to me and not charge a penny? Later, Esther reminded me of Jesus' promise in Mark 10:29-30: *Jesus answered and said, Verily I say unto you, There is no man that hath left house, or brethren, or sisters, or father, or mother, or wife, or children, or lands, for my sake, and the gospel's, But he shall receive an hundredfold now in this time, houses, and brethren, and sisters, and mothers, and children, and lands, with persecutions; and in the world to come eternal life.* This promise has held true for us many times since that first experience with the car owner. God has blessed our family a hundredfold, and then more.

My eyes were opened to the Bible like never before. The Sunday school teacher was Jerry Gess, and he taught our class verse by verse through the Bible. Those first three years were almost like a honeymoon. Esther and I just soaked it all in and grew continually stronger in our faith.

When I was young, many of the sermons I heard were centered around God the Father. Suddenly, I was going to a church where they mostly talked about the Son. I remember thinking, *The Father must be offended.* But after hearing many different sermons, I realized the importance of the Son's role, and how He, through death, burial, and resurrection, was able to bridge the huge gulf between us and God the Father.

My pastor, John Bouquet, took a liking to me and gave me three nice suits to wear at church. But he did much more. He sat down with Esther and me for multiple Bible studies and answered all our questions from the Word of God. It was so different from our old culture where the Bible was hardly ever used and most questions were answered with tradition and church rules. Eventually, we realized we needed to be baptized by immersion, which differed from the Amish teachings in a number of ways. Pastor John taught from the Word of God on who, when, why, and how a person should be baptized. He explained how the Greek word *baptizo* appears eighty times in the New Testament and always means to "put under or immerse." It wasn't something Esther and I had to do to become Christians but was something we wanted to do because we were Christians.

Colossians 2:12 says that we are *Buried with Him in baptism, wherein also ye are risen with Him through the faith of the operation of God, Who hath raised him from the dead.*

Our church had about 250 members, and many of them reached out to us. On the day we were baptized, we were the center of attention with everybody excited and praising the Lord for all He was doing in our young lives. Once baptism was behind us, we immediately wanted to become members of this local body of believers. Pastor John took us under his wing, and to this day, he is still the pastor, and we are still members.

Chapter 14

The Transition

Soon after Esther and I left the Amish, two ministers came to see us at the Gess home to pressure us to turn ourselves over to Satan. At first, they tried to stay away from having a scriptural debate, but as time went on, one shared the biblical account in 1 Corinthians 5:5-7 of the young man who had committed incest with his father's wife. In that case, the apostle Paul wrote to the church and asked them *To deliver such an one unto Satan for the destruction of the flesh, that the spirit may be saved in the day of the Lord Jesus. . . . Know ye not that a little leaven leaveneth the whole lump? Purge out therefore the old leaven, that ye may be a new lump, as ye are unleavened.*

As a young Christian, I wondered how anyone could put us in the same category as those who commit incest. Surely, changing cultures and attending a non-Amish church did not make us ungodly people.

The deacon cleared his throat and said, "We are requesting you to accept the ban on yourself so we, as a church, can deliver you up to Satan."

Up to this point, I had never had the nerve to speak up to

an Amish preacher, but I replied, "The blood is on you. If that's what you feel you have to do, you will answer to God."

After a few hours of pleading and begging us to return, the two preachers realized that Esther and I were not going to return to the Amish church. They struggled to accept our answers, and it was hard for us to see them take it so hard because they truly believed we were headed for the lake of fire.

Soon after we started attending Bethel Baptist Church, one of the members bought me a nice full-sized study Bible. For the next three years, I read that Bible through and through and absorbed and understood God's truth. I couldn't get enough of it. Even today, I am reminded that 1 Corinthians 2:9-10 is not something that takes place beyond the grave; it's happening now: *But as it is written, Eye hath not seen, nor ear heard, neither have entered into the heart of man, the things which God hath prepared for them that love him. But God hath revealed them unto us by his Spirit: for the Spirit searcheth all things, yea, the deep things of God.*

I highlighted verses and wrote notes all over the margins of my Bible, which eventually fell apart from use. I wanted to tell the whole world. I'd go up to complete strangers and ask, "If you died today are you sure you'd go to heaven?" I preached in nursing homes and went soul-winning every Thursday night.

One of the hardest things about leaving the Amish was leaving my family. Dad made it clear we weren't ever to set foot on his property. The inner turmoil former Amish feel as they are tugged between their love for their family and their love for following Jesus as the Truth of God is evident in "Dear Parents," an article written by a friend of mine:

> It's me. Your child. I want to tell you what's been on my heart for a while. You see, in spite of the fact that I've chosen a different life than you ever would have wanted

me to, it doesn't mean I dislike you. Just because I've chosen not to embrace your religion doesn't mean I don't embrace you. In spite of our differences, I want to tell you that I love you.

When my work is done for the day, I sit on my porch and ponder and pray. I know this may seem strange to you, since it must seem to you that I have chosen a path that leads away from God, but listen to what I have to say. You see, I pray for you two, because I love you, and because I know God loves you. I have faith that our relationship can be restored.

As I have pondered our relationship, I always wished to share my heart, but there is a bit of a barrier between us. No doubt it's been hard on you, this decision of mine to walk away from all you believe in. I can only imagine how you feel. I do know, though, that barriers can be torn down and tonight I've been given an answer to prayer by being able to write this letter to you.

My dear parents, when I left your church, I did so without giving you more information than I absolutely had to. No doubt it seemed as though I was a disgrace to you and the church. To make it worse, I felt as if I could tell you two nothing that would make you feel better. In fact, whenever I did tell you something, you seemed unable to even hear me. I'm so sorry – sorry that I didn't share more with you, spending time to make sure you understood exactly where I was coming from. Because, you see, I don't dislike you or anyone in the church. Please separate that from the fact that I cannot subscribe to the religion of your church. You must keep a handle on the fact that I love you but dislike your religion. You are not your religion; you are so much more.

My dear parents, if you want to know if I have a relationship with Christ, you must ask me. Please let this be a sign to me that you care and want to know where I stand with the Lord – by asking me to tell you more. Until I know that you want to hear about my relationship with the Lord, I will have a hard time sharing. You two are still my parents, and the fact that you tell me how wrong I am makes it harder for me to share my true love, my relationship with my Lord.

It is very puzzling to me that you ask me often if I belong to a church, but don't ask me if I have a relationship with God. I fear that you think more highly of your church than you do of God. I cling to a faint hope that we are merely misunderstanding each other, and that we are merely dancing around each other, never getting to the core of matters. When you do care to hear me out, I will gladly share, and perhaps we can gain some common ground.

I do know that we have a common goal. We all want to go to heaven, to eternally worship and be with God, who is our perfect Creator. I also know that I don't have a leg to stand on myself, having absolutely no righteousness. Only God is righteous, and I claim Him as my own righteousness – and serve Him out of love and faith in what He has done for me. Oh my dear parents, do not think I am casting away my love of God by leaving your traditions. Rather, I am leaving your traditions because they were a stumbling block to me, just as they were to the Jews in Jesus' time. My prayer is that you will not trip on the same stumbling block, though I fear it may be so.

Above all, please know that I am praying for you and will wait patiently until you openly ask me questions regarding my faith. Until then, I am praying that you will understand that I am not holding myself above you in earthly standards; rather, I am openly confessing that I am nothing. I reserve nothing for myself, only desiring to serve God who is my Savior. Until then, I will think back over my childhood and remember all you have done for me. I am so thankful that you are my parents, because I love you and know that you gave so much to me. Until then, my dear parents, remember that God loves you.

Your son

———————

One Sunday evening, about a year after we left, I asked Esther to drive me out to my parents' place.

"Drop me off at the end of the driveway. We won't park our vehicle on their property, and I'll see if Dad and Mom will accept me."

I really didn't know what to expect as I got out of the car and headed down the lane to what had been my home. To my surprise, my family was very happy to see me.

We sat talking and everything was going well until someone knocked at the door. Dad stood up and said, "Run, Joe, run, hide. I don't want anyone to know you are in the house."

I darted from the kitchen into the living room and through the door to my parents' bedroom. The Amish people came in, talked for a while, and left.

I came out of hiding, and we talked more. Another knock at the door. More Amish people. Dad was still a busy man. Again, he said, "Run!" and I did.

Again, I hid, but this time they didn't leave. I stayed hidden for a half hour and knew Esther would be arriving soon to pick me up. So, I opened my parents' bedroom window and crawled out. Sadly, I was not able to say goodbye.

While leaving the Amish was very hard, fitting in with another culture was and still is very hard. We were rejected by our culture, so we could no longer consider ourselves Amish. We'd joined the English culture, but we weren't born in the English culture. It was like a US citizen going to another country and learning a different manner of dress, but always feeling a bit like an outsider. This is a common sentiment among the ones who dangle between Amish and English culture. Sometimes it bogs us down and the only people we can relate to are former Amish.

For example, in my home church we have quite a few former Amish. They all sit together in one corner. Often, when the other people go home, the former Amish linger to talk and catch up. We hold a fellowship meal every other Sunday, mostly for former Amish but we also invite English to join us.

Another difficulty former Amish face, particularly the young men, is going into debt. They get jobs and start earning weekly paychecks. The first thing they want is a big four-wheel-drive extended cab truck. Then they modify the muffler, buy bigger speakers, and add fancy rims. Suddenly, they are unable to pay their insurance and upkeep and many other expenses that come with the English lifestyle.

Transitions filter into religious and social aspects of life too. After attending the Baptist church for about two years, my pastor came and asked if I wanted to be a deacon. For me, that meant the lot fell on me. They just came and asked me. I felt awkward and started thinking of family and others – what would they think of me being a self-appointed deacon? After thinking and praying about becoming a deacon, I accepted the invitation to start out as a deacon-in-training for one year.

In the Amish culture, we only had one deacon per church district. In the English culture, or at least at Bethel, we always had eight or more deacons. What the pastor and deacons didn't realize was that sitting in a group of older men every month and discussing things was huge for me. For that first year, I said very little and just observed. Whenever it felt appropriate, I nodded my head and said yea when asked to vote. During one of our meetings, we discussed the need to fix potholes in our church driveway. Immediately, my thoughts went back to childhood; I remembered the potholes in our driveway and how we'd get our pickaxes, cut a rectangular hole about two inches deep, and lay brick in there with gravel over it. It worked! The pothole never came back.

I waited for a moment of silence and then shared my experience with potholes.

"Well, go get the pickaxe and start hacking away," my pastor said with a laugh.

He didn't realize it had taken me a year to say something. When he laughed, everybody laughed. I thought I was going to die. I went to the chairman that night and said, "I'm done. I can't handle this."

The next day, he went to my pastor and told him what had happened. In thirty years, I've seen my pastor cry a few times, and that was one of them. Tears pooled in his eyes and spilled down his cheeks as he apologized. At the time, it was a big deal for me, and we both learned from that. Afterward, he encouraged me to stay on the board. I did stay and served as a deacon for the next twenty years. Several years in a row, the older deacons asked me to serve as the chairman of the board. I accepted it with honor and a humble heart.

There's a mindset among the Amish that differs from the

English way of thinking. We worked hard at doing community. Large groups of people often gathered at someone's property to help with the bigger projects. We were known as the people who could raise a huge barn in one day. The women, on the other hand, got together monthly and helped each other with canning and housecleaning.

The most difficult adjustment for us in the English world, was the equal status of men and women. In the Amish culture the men always led, and everyone knew it. Unfortunately, this sometimes resulted in abusive situations. The men were harsh with their authority – not just at home but in the church. The women could vote in the church, but they voted in agreement with the men. In one case, my sister voted against the men. The next day, three ministers from the church were at her doorstep. She could either revoke her vote or they were going to publicly discipline her in front of the church. She revoked her vote. In the English culture, men and women are more equal. Not only are women occupying church positions, but they also serve as doctors, lawyers, police, and judges.

Another big area of difference in our cultures is dress code standards. Amish women dressed so they were covered from top to bottom. Dresses were to reach within a certain number of inches from the ground and all the way up to the neckline. Men and women weren't even allowed to have short sleeves, and we wore head coverings and hats. About the only things that stuck out were our hands and faces. For several years after we left the Amish culture, I emphasized a strict dress code for Esther and our daughter, Rachel. I did so mostly because I saw where the rest of society was headed. Women's clothing styles are often skin tight and revealing, even in the church. It still is very difficult for me to accept, but I've also learned that some things you just can't change.

Chapter 15

Family

After our stay with Jerry and Carol Gess, we had enough money for a deposit and first month's rent on a small one-bedroom house. We didn't have any children, but eventually the concept of paying someone rent felt like wasted money, and we started looking for our own house. Within a few months, we found one that had two bedrooms. We gathered all our savings together and put a bid on the house.

The only way to borrow money is the bank, I remember thinking. *What if we fall flat on our faces and can't make the payments? We don't have our Amish community to fall back on.* It was scary and a huge deal for Esther and me.

We lived in that house for ten years. Our children, Jonathan and Rachel, were born during that time, and I worked third shift as a tool and die maker while Esther homeschooled our children. Jonathan was homeschooled all the way through and Rachel was homeschooled until 6th grade. After that, she decided homeschool was no longer working for her, so for one year, we let her go to public school, but that didn't work so well either. The following year, we found a private Christian school we could afford. It was at this school that Rachel continued to blossom and mature into a beautiful young lady.

A personal blessing came from Rachel attending Mansfield Temple Christian when she entered a Father's Day letter-writing contest and won first prize. As a result of getting first prize, she and I were allowed to walk the red carpet. I shared her letter in Appendix A with a humble heart and give God all the glory He alone deserves.

When our children were still young, Esther and I often talked about how we might raise them differently from how we were raised. When I saw my pastor, in his forties, hug and kiss his parents goodnight, I went straight to Esther and shared how I'd like to incorporate that into our family, and we did. To this day, our family always hugs and kisses when we separate and go our own ways. We tell them how much they are loved and valued.

Jonathan decided he was not going to attend college. Instead, at the age of seventeen he reached out to a company in Phoenix, Arizona, and got a job working through the Internet. He worked from home and became very successful. The fellow he worked for had no idea he was only seventeen, so when the owner of the company wanted him to fly out to Phoenix for an investor conference, Jonathan quickly became worried. He thought meeting face-to-face could cost him the job. Not only was he underage, but he felt his short stature and considerably youthful appearance could cost him the job.

Jonathan bought a brand-new suit, necktie, and shoes for the conference his boss wanted him to attend. Our entire family started praying that God would work things out for him, and He did. The same day he turned eighteen, he got on a plane in Cleveland, Ohio, and flew to Arizona. He appeared grown up and confident, and we couldn't have been more proud of him. His boss, also the owner of the company, loved Jonathan regardless of his stature or how he looked to the others at the conference. Jonathan has since launched a few more companies with the owner and is doing very well as second-in-command.

Jonathan's entrepreneurial spirit doesn't allow him to sit idle. He runs several side businesses that he developed from the ground up and has multiple employees scattered throughout the United States. He paid his first house off by the time he was twenty-three and he bought a second one just five houses up from ours. In all his businesses, he still finds time to be faithfully involved in the lives of young people on Wednesday nights at our home church. He has a passion to help young people succeed in life and has invested many hours mentoring and discipling them.

When our children were ten years old, we read through a series of four books written by Stan and Brenda Jones. Each book explained in detail how God designed the human body and how their young bodies would change as they grew older. By the time they reached twelve, both Jonathan and Rachel knew all about the birds and bees. We left no stone unturned.

We often discussed the future with our children and how they would at some point in their teenage years try to pull away from us, and we made plans on how to handle those difficult times. Those difficult teenage times did come along and some were brutal, but now we can look back and say we were ready and prepared. Most were handled right, and many years of pain were eliminated.

At our house, we have a prayer couch in the living room, and every morning we sat down with Jonathan and Rachel individually and prayed over them. When we got done praying for them, they returned the favor and prayed over us. We often prayed that God would help them to stay sexually pure during their dating years and bring them a godly spouse. We made purity and godly spouses a huge deal, and so did Jonathan and Rachel.

When Rachel was sixteen, she said, "I'd like to put together a little ceremony for our close friends to whom I can be accountable and who would pray over me and read scriptures focusing on purity."

When the special day arrived, she made breakfast for everyone, and then about eight of us gathered in the living room. We each shared our heart with Rachel, read Scripture, and in the end, we laid hands on her and asked God to give her wisdom and bless and protect her. She slipped a purity ring on her finger and made a vow before God and us that she would stay pure. Finally, we signed a certificate that was framed and hung in her room. Next to the certificate was a picture frame with a silhouette of a man.

When Rachel met David at Bible college, she told him they couldn't date until he met five requirements. The first was to meet with Dad; David was okay with that, so the plans for a face-to-face meeting were made.

The day Esther and I went to meet David, I took a list of questions along. Rachel and our pastor had approved the questions. I was determined that he had to be clean cut, born again, on fire for the Lord, and hopefully raised in a solid Christian home where family was a priority.

When we arrived at Malone University, Rachel met us in the parking lot.

"Dad, I trust you, but act normal and *please* be gentle – it's not like we are looking to become engaged."

"Don't worry, Betsy (Rachel's childhood nickname), just pray that I can capture the roaring lion within me and leave him behind."

No doubt, I was sweating and my heart was pumping double as David and I headed for the Red Lobster. Plans were that Esther and Rachel would spend some mother-daughter time, while I grilled poor David.

We sat down and both ordered the Ultimate Feast.

"Okay, David, now that we are sitting here waiting on the food, I want you to know it's not easy for this daddy to let just anybody take my Betsy away. Before Rachel was born, her mom and I began to pray that God would bring the right man into her life. Now that it appears we have come to that point in our journey, I would like to ask you a few questions."

I proceeded to work through my lengthy list, which can be found in Appendix B.

In the end, I felt very comfortable with David, and I trusted Rachel. But this was just the first step. David had to meet four more of Rachel's requirements.

Over the next two years, David and Rachel read seven books on dating and marriage while she finished four years of college in three. Her desire was to graduate at about the same time as David, who had started a year earlier. Not only did our family feel like we gained a son, we also became very close friends with David's parents. Truly, the Lord honored our labor and blessed us beyond comprehension.

When David asked to meet with Esther and me, we had a gut feeling that it was going to be a request to marry Rachel. We had already decided that David was God's chosen man and he belonged in the picture frame in Rachel's bedroom. But before we just answered yes, I said, "David, we have been preparing for this time and have a few comments and another list of questions we would like to ask you."

This list was even longer than the first, but David understood our concern and the importance of doing what was right. This list can be found in Appendix C.

Esther and I had made a big deal of dating, purity, and marriage, and because we made a big deal of it, so did our children. David and Rachel married a few months later, and I had the privilege of doing the wedding vows with them. I cried like a baby that day as I walked our Betsy down the aisle and gave her hand away to a man I had only known for two years. They were tears of sadness, joy, and probably about twenty other emotions.

About a year went by and Rachel became pregnant with Squirt, or so we called her until she got her real name, Lily. Recently, we heard the good news that Rachel is pregnant again, this time it's a little boy who goes by the name Sprout.

Jonathan was more independent. Jonathan wasn't comfortable with doing a ceremony, but we did purchase a watch with "purity" engraved on the back of it in place of a purity ring. He moved out at nineteen and bought his own house. He's always done very well with his finances, but at twenty-six he was struggling emotionally. However, that served as an epiphany for him. He was stuck out in North Dakota, trying to prove a new business model involving hail storms and home restoration, but it wasn't going like he planned.

When he returned home, he said, "My life is going to change drastically. I'm going to find myself a girlfriend."

The first gal didn't work out, but he wasn't about to give up. A few weeks went by, and a friend of ours connected him with Havilah. They are in love and now taking some of the same steps David and Rachel did.

Since Jonathan lives just down the street from us, he comes home a couple night a week and eats supper with us. It makes mamma shine and fills Jonathan's heart with gladness! Now that he's been dating Havilah, she comes home with him for supper several nights a week. We've really grown fond of her.

One Monday night when we went out for family night, Jonathan said, "Well Dad, you'd be proud of me. I sat down and wrote a letter and asked Havilah's father if he'd allow me to start a relationship with his daughter."

He did it on his own, and I was so proud of him.

He got a very positive response back. Her father said, "By

all means you have my permission. We are excited for your life and Havilah's life."

Today, both of our adult children are involved in their home churches. Jonathan teaches the youth on Wednesday nights and has a heart to mentor people who have grown up in broken homes. David and Rachel lead a Monday night Bible study at their home and work with childcare.

I have no greater joy than to hear that my children walk in truth. (3 John 4)

Chapter 16

God's Call

For fifteen years after leaving the Amish, I stayed away from them. I minded my own business and became involved in ministry at my church. I enjoyed opportunities to preach in nursing homes and took part in soul winning every Thursday night. As time went on, the church asked if I would teach the fourth, fifth, and sixth grade boys during Sunday school. For five years, I poured my life into fifteen young boys whom I became very attached to. Not only did we spend time in the classroom, but we got together during the week and did fun stuff. Several of the boys came from broken homes and needed a father figure in their lives. God used me to fill that gap, and it made me feel as though I was making a difference.

Eventually, our youth pastor decided I should move to the teenage Sunday school class. Many of the same boys who were in my earlier class moved with me, and God gave me a few more years to teach and equip them for life. Three of those young boys are now in full-time ministry. Aaron pastors a church in Tennessee, Matt pastors a church plant in Vermont, and Mike is a college professor and has served in various Christian colleges in the US. I couldn't be more proud of them, and have always praised God for the small part I had in their lives.

One year at a missions conference in my home church, John Jackson spoke from Monday through Wednesday. On Tuesday night, I felt as if he was speaking directly to me. I remember getting out of my seat and going forward. I knew God was calling me into the ministry. Kenny, one of the pastors, came up and put his arm around me.

"Why did you come to the altar?"

"Tonight, I surrender my whole heart and soul to God," I said. "I'll go to Africa or wherever God wants me to go."

I wasn't thinking about going to the Amish, though. There was no ministry like that, and besides, I felt the same way Jonah did about Nineveh – the less I had to do with the Amish, the better.

A couple of years went by, and I found myself thinking about the Amish on a regular basis. More and more young boys were leaving the culture, and at one time, we had three boys living in our two-bedroom house. They were sleeping on our couch and on the floor. Esther and I realized there was a need.

Then I learned of an Amish man who had committed suicide in Mount Eaton, Ohio. He left a wife and three children behind. Esther and I decided to go to the viewing. When we got there, we learned that this was the third suicide in that community in a year. Most Amish believe that if someone commits suicide, they can't go to heaven. In some communities, members who commit suicide are buried outside the cemetery fence without a headstone. Within a few years, no one can tell where the person was buried. This happened with the three who committed suicide in this Mount Eaton community.

Esther and I walked into that house to find the women all huddled in the kitchen, dressed in black, while the men gathered in the living room. No one talked. It was very dark and gloomy – hopeless. They brought us into a room lit with

a kerosene lamp. A man lay on his back on two-by-six boards with white linen pulled up to his neck. Shadows danced on the walls and across the body as the lamplight flickered. For the first time, it really tore me up to think that flame from the lamp was nothing compared to the flames of hell. I asked myself, *Who is going to tell these people there is hope?* This man committed suicide because if he left the Amish church, he'd be excommunicated and turned over to Satan. If he stayed, he couldn't cope with it. The only way out was to go upstairs and shoot himself in the head.

I walked out of that house into the pitch darkness. I'd almost forgotten how black the nights are without electricity. On the way home I said to Esther, "Somebody has to tell these people about the gospel."

For the next six months, I suffered through turmoil at work. I woke up in the morning and cried all the way to work. Not because of my job – I loved my work – but because of the hopelessness in the Amish community. I prayed God would send someone to the Amish culture. I didn't think it was me. It couldn't be me – I was excommunicated from the Amish church, despised and judged as a rebel, and considered a lost soul headed for hell.

Time went on and the inner struggles became unbearable. While at work one day, I walked to the restroom, locked myself in a stall, and wept bitterly.

"God, what are You trying to do with me?" I cried. "I can't take this anymore. Please! Just take my life."

John, a Christian brother, walked in and stepped into the next stall. He started singing a Christian song to comfort me. He was fully aware that I was at war with God.

Finally, I said, "John, leave. I want you to leave me alone."

I walked out, and John said, "Joe, you need to go to your pastor and tell him what you're going through."

I took that advice, and a week later I met with my pastor at Perkins restaurant.

"Pastor, I have one question. What does it feel like when God calls a person into the ministry? How is one supposed to know it's God?"

His answer was exactly what I needed to hear. "Joe, I've watched you for fifteen years, and I know the Lord has His hand on you. I've been waiting for this moment. In fact, I already have a name for your ministry – Mission to Amish People."

For me, this was a huge confirmation, but I didn't want to go to the Amish. I didn't want to offend them, and I was worried about what they would do to me.

I asked, "So what is a missionary to the Amish supposed to do?"

He smiled. "Don't worry about those details."

He encouraged me to let the church know what God was doing in my life. On February 6, 2000, I stood in front of my home church and preached the morning service from Romans 10:1-4;

> Brethren, my heart's desire and prayer to God for
> Israel is, that they might be saved. For I bear them
> record that they have a zeal of God, but not accord-
> ing to knowledge. For they being ignorant of God's
> righteousness, and going about to establish their own
> righteousness, have not submitted themselves unto
> the righteousness of God. For Christ is the end of the
> law for righteousness to every one that believeth.

"That they might be saved," I repeated thoughtfully as I looked out at the congregation of familiar faces. "My heart's desire for the Amish is that they might be saved." I talked about their deception regarding their *own righteousness*.

Then I turned to Romans 9:3. *For I could wish that myself were accursed from Christ for my brethren, my kinsmen according to the flesh.* Tears stung my eyes. "If possible I would be accursed," I said. I tapped the page with my index finger. "That's me. I can't get away from it. All I can think about day and night is my people." I swallowed hard trying to clear the emotional lump in my throat.

I closed with Acts chapter 10 and said, "Peter, who was a Jew, went to the home of Cornelius who was a Gentile, and Gentiles also became believers. As a former Amish man, serving among the English people for fifteen years, we must go to the Amish with the pure gospel of Jesus Christ and tell them the truth."

I believed with all my heart that part of our ministry was going to be about bringing an awareness about the Amish to Bible-preaching churches.

When I finished, my pastor stepped up to the podium and said, "Church, I want you to get behind the Keim family, because they are going to go to other churches just like other missionaries and raise support to go full time."

My home church got behind us, and to this day they have given tens of thousands of dollars. Most of the people who signed up to give that day still give today – every month.

I had invited some former Amish to come that day, and about fifty attended from all over, including some from Kentucky, Indiana, Tennessee, and Ohio. That's how MAP Ministry (Mission to Amish People) started.

Within a few weeks, Esther and I met with Pastor John and his wife, Sherry, and came up with a ministry presentation outline that could be used at churches. It started with sharing our testimony and included our burden, what the Amish believe, and how we were going to reach out. We still follow the same outline or variation of it, and we've spoken in more than five hundred churches all over America.

Churches came on board one after another, and by April 1, 2001, we had enough money pledged and coming in that we felt we could go full time. I left my secular job as a tool and die maker, and I made my office in a little Sunday school room at my home church. Going into ministry meant my salary would be cut in half, but Esther and I knew, without a doubt, we were following God's call and approached the change in faith and did our part. Esther worked a full-time job so we could have insurance, because my salary wasn't enough to afford that expense.

In the early years of the ministry, when I'd go out and speak in churches, I'd leave an evaluation sheet with the pastor. He could then evaluate and let us know whether they would help support us. I'll never forget one pastor's evaluation. "Good on his presentation but could brush up on his English."

Comments like this put me into a tailspin. I only had an eighth-grade education. Most pastors have at least a four-year degree. For many years, if someone asked where I got my education, I'd beat around the bush because I didn't want people to know I was uneducated.

However, the feelings of having a lesser education have changed in the last few years. God reminded me that He chose uneducated fishermen to be His disciples, and truthfully, if I had a choice of being well educated or being filled and overflowing with the Spirit of God, I'd choose the Spirit and power of God any time. Many people sit in our church pews, thinking they must first get Bible training before they can be used by God. That is a false belief!

God often uses us the most in our weaknesses. Many times, I nearly fainted when asked to pray in front of the congregation. Never in a million years did I think God would use me to speak in so many churches. God just wants willing hearts who fully surrender themselves to Him. He'll take it from there. Esther and I are living proof!

Now when they saw the boldness of Peter and John,

and perceived that they were unlearned and igno-
rant men, they marvelled; and they took knowledge
of them, that they had been with Jesus. (Acts 4:13)

The ministry has grown every year since 2000, when we first presented our burden and vision to our home church. In our first full-time year, we furnished a Sunday school room with a desk, computer, and phone. We eventually expanded to a second Sunday school room and hired a secretary. Volunteers joined us. We moved into a third room and even that became tight. We went out back and built a 2,000-square-foot building. In 2013 we added on 1,500 square feet. Today, we have about twelve computers and twelve desks, six staff members, and fifty volunteers who work for this ministry. Many churches in this area give thousands of hours. It's just amazing. And people love it. Many are retired, and some work three eight-hour days every week. They love coming to MAP and serving the Lord. I can't tell you what a blessing they are in the Lord's work.

I knew I wasn't going to be a normal missionary, because most missionaries go and live among the people they are trying to reach. That approach would not work for us and the people we are trying to reach. Not everyone understands this, and I have people call me and say, "We have groups that go on short-term mission trips for two weeks." While we'd like to have groups come and join us, our mission is completely different.

Chapter 17

How Do We Reach Out, Lord?

With much prayer, we considered various ways to reach out, but we recognized our limitations. We wouldn't be able to have a TV or radio ministry because the Amish can't have electronic devices. We couldn't even reach out through the Internet. As we prayed and brainstormed, Esther came up with a great idea that has turned into the biggest ministry we have.

Early in our walk with the Lord, Esther and I received correspondence Bible lessons out of Georgia. We even studied those lessons with our children for several years. God brought this experience to mind as we talked about ways to reach the Amish.

Esther said, "They don't have TV, radio, or Internet, but they all have a mailbox."

We gathered up Amish directories and went through lists of at least 50,000 Amish families. From each family, we chose one person and mailed them lesson number one. If the person who received the Bible lesson took the test and sent it back, we graded it, made some personal notes, and sent it back with lesson two. Since our first Bible lessons went out in 2001, more than 35,000 individuals have enrolled in a Bible course. Over time, some dropped off the rolls, and new ones enrolled. At this time, we are running about 5,000 active students.

The Bible Club offers forty-five courses with materials available for children from age five up through adults. Special courses aimed at teens include topics such as love, dating, and marriage. In addition, we offer about ten in-depth courses through the Plowman's Academy. Each of these courses can take up to six months to complete. In all, we've seen more than 2,500 salvation decisions come back in the mail.

Both the Bible Club and Plowman's Academy are evangelistic and discipleship outreaches. The materials explain God's plan of salvation over and over. Most who make decisions are older children, but we also have some adults. Some who've been saved through the Bible Club have gone on to Bible college.

Who is Your Nineveh?

Iva, an Amish girl from Indiana, surrendered her life to Christ after doing a Bible study course. She then felt led to enroll in a Bible school in Pennsylvania. She packed her clothes, got on the train, and traveled to Pennsylvania to begin two years of Bible school. Toward the end of her second year, she heard a sermon preached on Jonah and his refusal to go to Nineveh.

When the evangelist ended his sermon, he asked, "Who is your Nineveh?"

Iva knew in her heart that her Nineveh was her own people, the Amish population. That night she went forward and surrendered to God's call. A few days later, she found our ministry on the Internet and figured out we were the ones who sent her the Bible Club lessons. After a few phone calls and a face-to-face meeting, Iva joined MAP and served with us for six months before she married a former-Amish missionary and moved away.

Others who have been saved through the Bible Club chose to stay in the Amish culture and have gone on to become preachers in the church. Without a doubt, God is doing a work among our people that is far beyond our comprehension. He's using an army of prayer warriors, donors, and volunteers that stretches across North America and other parts of the world.

God had been preparing Esther and me for this ministry as we had been helping those trying to leave the Amish for a long time. Our first had been a young man, Harvey, who called us from Wisconsin. He wanted to leave the Amish and needed a place to stay while he got on his feet.

"I got a bus ticket," he said.

He rode in that Greyhound more than a day, and I waited at the bus station on the other end. The bus pulled up amid the smell of diesel fumes. Passengers started funneling out. They kept coming and coming, and I watched for an Amish-looking man but didn't see one. When the bus sat empty, I wondered what happened to Harvey. Suddenly, a guy walked toward me, dressed totally in camouflage and carrying two shotguns that were hidden in blankets. It was Harvey! Along with the little money in his pocket, those guns were all he had. I wondered, *How in the world did he get those guns on the bus?*

Since then, we have taken in over 150 individuals and families who left the Amish and needed immediate shelter and help to transition. Out of those 150, one was my brother William. My brothers, Johnny and Perry, also left the Amish, but they lived with other people.

On many occasions, our dad has reminded each one of us that our marriages will very likely end in divorce. Then he'd add, "I've seen it happen over and over."

He also pointed out in many of his letters that we brothers would eventually fall away from church and our children would end up not believing anything. Since he made these remarks with such confidence, we worried and wondered if our dad might be right.

However, we also believed that with God's help, these things would not come true. Today, each one of our four families is still actively attending and involved in our local church. By God's wonderful grace and mercy, all our children are living for the Lord, while the older ones are serving in various ministries.

This has taught us several things: (1) If someone predicts your future failures, don't argue. You don't have to prove anything to anybody. Just stay focused and keep walking with the Lord. (2) Just because others have left the Amish and failed doesn't mean I will fail. (3) Our testimonies always speak for themselves.

Lessons to be Learned

A young girl named Elizabeth came to MAP from a Schwart-zentruber sect in Tennessee. She barely spoke English when we first took her in. We helped her get a birth certificate, Social Security number, and finally a job where Esther worked. Elizabeth was excited about her new job and could hardly wait to get started. About half-way through her shift, Esther glanced over and noticed that some of the employees were giggling and whispering behind Elizabeth's back. One of the employees even picked up a spray can and sprayed above Elizabeth's head, and the giggling continued.

What the employees didn't realize was that Elizabeth was from a different culture that did not allow deodorant or shaving legs and armpits and they only took one bath a week. Suddenly two cultures clashed in the workplace, and by day two Elizabeth was let go by the company.

Elizabeth refused to let the incident stop her from moving forward. She learned from her first job and moved on to another. She decided to get her GED (General Education Development) certificate, which took about two years to finish. Sometimes she wanted to give up, but we kept encouraging her to persevere, and the day she graduated, we celebrated and told her how proud we were of her accomplishments. Elizabeth went on to nursing school at a local university and graduated in 2016.

Esther and I have had to sit down with many adults over the years and teach them the basics of English culture, such as using deodorant, matching colors in clothing, shaving legs and armpits, brushing teeth, leaving tips for the waitress, operating electrical appliances, and changing into a clean set of clothes daily. This process is uncomfortable for everybody and often feels like parents talking to their five-year-old child. Some must be taught simple manners, such as saying thank you, holding the door for others, and using the word *please*. Others have to be taught that opening the refrigerator, eating out of ice cream boxes, and drinking from milk jugs before returning them to the fridge is a no-no.

Before I go any further, let me say that these are mostly issues with those coming out of the ultra-conservative groups. The more liberal Amish know about hygiene and have been taught better manners. They have a much easier time transitioning into English culture.

Samuel

In 2012, an Amish man from Indiana moved into our home and wanted us to help him make the transition. About six months earlier, someone had given Samuel Girod my number, and he decided to hang on to it, thinking it might come in handy someday. Late one afternoon, he took his forbidden cell phone and walked out behind the barn so no one could see him. He was thirty years old. Later he told me, "I shook like a leaf when I punched your number in the phone."

Not only was he using a phone he wasn't supposed to own, but he was calling an ex-Amish man who had been excommunicated from the church. His dad was a bishop, which made it even more important for Samuel to follow the rules of the church.

Today Samuel says, "Joe, I'll never forget that first conversation I had with you. I thought you'd tell me to leave the Amish. Instead, you just sat back and listened, which is exactly what I needed at that moment."

Samuel shared some of the turmoil he was facing in his Swiss Amish community. When we finished talking, he asked, "Is it okay for me to call you again?"

"Of course, Samuel! You can call me anytime."

Six months went by. During this time, Samuel called every couple of weeks. Some days he wanted to leave the Amish, but within hours, he'd change his mind.

I did not try to persuade Samuel in any direction, but only cared for his heart and tried to encourage him as much as possible. Truthfully, I didn't think he'd ever leave the Amish.

But then, he called again. "I'm leaving the Amish!"

I could hear determination in his voice – determination I knew so well on a personal level.

"Here I am at thirty years old, co-owner of a construction business. I own two properties, I don't have a wife, and I'm utterly miserable," he said.

Samuel belonged to a Swiss Amish group that didn't allow members to get a wife outside of their own sect. In Samuel's case, there weren't enough ladies left over for him to get married and have his own family. He was totally miserable.

"I just can't continue to live this way any longer," he said.

On September 22, 2012, Samuel left everything – his business, properties, family, culture, and community. He just closed the door, walked for several miles in the dark so no one would see him leave, got a taxi, and showed up at our place in Ohio on Sunday morning with two duffel bags. For the next two days, we sat in my office and covered scripture after scripture.

"Samuel, salvation does not come from belonging to a certain culture; it's not a list of dos and don'ts that makes the heart of a human being right with God. Salvation only comes by God's grace through faith," I said. *For by grace are ye saved through faith; and that not of yourselves: it is the gift of God: Not of works, lest any man should boast* (Ephesians 2:8-9).

I will never forget. It was all so precious. We were sitting in my office for the second day in a row, covering God's simple plan of salvation, when suddenly the Holy Spirit of God opened Samuel's deaf ears and his spiritual eyes to the truth. A once dead and ignorant Samuel shouted out, "I get it!" It was so like my own experience on July 28, 1985.

When Samuel called on the name of the Lord for salvation, God totally transformed him from the inside out. He turned into a totally different person. Before his transformation took place, his eyes were filled with torment and pain. When Christ came into his life, all that changed immediately, right before our eyes. He was instantly filled with peace.

We helped Samuel get his driver's license. He bought a truck and a smartphone, and he lived with us for a while. Before long he found out about a former Amish lady who had left her community much the same way he did. Polly was about his age and was also looking for a man, preferably former Amish who would understand her ways. Within two months they were married. Today Samuel and Polly are missionaries with MAP. They travel all over the country, speaking in churches and encouraging former Amish to continue in the faith.

In 2016, Samuel became an ordained preacher by his home church, Hope Baptist Church in Indiana. He loves to preach and is continually burdened to reach his family and other Amish people who do not understand the true gospel of Jesus Christ.

Unsuccessful Contacts

Though we have been able to help many of those who come to us, not every case ends up being a success story. We took in a young man who traveled all the way from Texas. Mario was twenty-two years old and very depressed when he found our ministry on the Internet. For the most part, we communicated via email. He was just three years old when his mom passed away, and shortly after, his dad left the Amish community in Ohio and moved out west with Mario. For some reason, his dad never got a birth certificate for him, and in time, the relationship between father and son completely deteriorated.

When I first heard from Mario, he sounded desperate. In one of his emails, he wrote:

> I will be around 23 and a half by the time I get my birth certificate, and I will barely be starting school, and I will be fighting for so many other things, I could just cry, thinking about all the wasted time. I feel so useless. I feel so worthless. I feel like just lying in bed, pulling up the covers, and just shutting off my brain forever. I don't want to think any longer. I feel like giving up because I am so tired of fighting, I don't want to fight anymore. ALL my entire life has been spent fighting, I am so worn out, Joe, and I want SO badly for just someone to take me in their arms and just let me cry there, for them to tell me that it's going to be alright, but I can't. I don't like people to see weakness in me, and I am terrified of being pitied, I feel like if I were to do something like that, that person would pity me and feel sorry for me and for all my struggles, and I don't want that. I've worked and fought so hard all my life to ever deserve the pity of anyone. But I am DYING inside, I want so badly to just scream forever.
>
> Please Joe, pray for me. I feel so lost, so stressed, and I feel such a dark sadness washing over me. You are one

of the only people I can confide in with these things. Nobody else knows what I'm going through besides you, I have found a trust in you I have found in no one else. I feel like I can tell you everything.

For over a year, I encouraged Mario to come to Ohio, so we could go down to Holmes County to see if we could find his Amish family and perhaps get started on a birth certificate. Finally, in 2012, Mario had saved up enough money for a Greyhound bus ticket to come to Mansfield, Ohio. We immediately got in the car and traveled to Holmes County and began our search for his family. Since he didn't know what Amish sect he was from, we checked in with the New Order, Old Order, and Schwartzentruber. No one knew about Mario or his family. Not a single Amish person was able to help, which devastated Mario even more.

One night, as we sat in Dairy Queen in Ashland, Ohio, Mario broke out in sobs. He wept so bitterly that his head and shoulders shook all over. I honestly did not know what to do, and a feeling of helplessness came over me.

Finally, Mario looked up at me and exclaimed, "In the eyes of the world, I don't exist. I'm a nobody."

Mario went back to Texas without a birth record.

Every week, we get phone calls and emails from those who have left Amish communities and need birth records, photo IDs, and Social Security numbers. The stories are all so familiar, "I tried to get my birth certificate, but they require a photo ID. Then I tried to get a photo ID, but that requires a birth certificate and a Social Security number. When I went to the Social Security office, I was informed I first need a photo ID and a birth certificate."

For some, this game goes on for several years, while they

meet with lawyers and judges and spend thousands of dollars. As a ministry, we have contacted our state representative and congressman, asking for help. Most of the time, they are not able to help. It's heartbreaking, and at times, people have broken down like Mario and wept. These are all lifelong American citizens in good standing, but they cannot get a driver's license, open bank accounts, or get jobs until they have a Social Security number.

The parents of these former Amish who are seeking birth records and Social Security numbers often refuse to provide any help or information. They hope their son or daughter will not be able to make it in the English culture and be forced to return to the Amish community.

Chapter 18

Former-Amish Church

One day a non-Amish veterinarian came to Sam Schwartz's house to check on a sick horse. The veterinarian was a Christian and asked Sam questions that eventually led to Sam placing his faith in Jesus Christ. Since Sam and his family only lived forty-five minutes from us, I went to visit them. Before long, it became clear that Sam, Laura, and their four young children were going to leave the Amish church. Sam got his driver's license and bought a car.

Not only was I concerned about helping them with physical needs but with their spiritual needs as well. One Saturday evening, I called Sam and asked, "Where are you going to church tomorrow?"

He said, "I was thinking I'd drive to the end of the driveway, and if God tells me left, I'll turn left. If He says right, I'll go right."

I said, "Sam, there are so many churches." I knew the importance of a sound Christian foundation. "Do you mind if Esther and I come to your place in the morning? We can have a church service in your house."

Sam didn't hesitate. "I would love that."

We started meeting every Sunday. Before long, more people joined us. Some were English neighbors, and others were Amish people who still attended the Amish church but secretly stopped by and participated in our Bible studies.

In time, some of Sam's family got saved, including his father, Levi. We decided to move the Sunday morning Bible study to Levi's house. When the house grew so full we couldn't meet there anymore, we moved into Levi's shop. Duct tape covered the cracks in the floor, and an old wood stove kept us warm. The first year we saw many get saved and about forty people were baptized. They were coming from all directions.

Our congregation was very colorful and from all backgrounds. Some drove all the way from Columbus, Ohio, and wore nose and tongue rings and had tattoos all over their bodies. Others came from an Amish background and still wore their plain clothes. It didn't matter to me what they looked like or where they came from. I was just excited that God had chosen me to preach the gospel and be their pastor. Those were some really exciting times.

When word got out that some Amish had left their church, various non-Amish denominations offered to lead Bible studies, often during the week when I wasn't around. Not all of these "Bible studies" were focused on the truth. We had Jehovah's Witnesses, Church of Christ, Mormons, Baptists, charismatics, and others. We also had ultra-conservative groups come that wanted to push head coverings and long dresses. Confusion grew. People questioned what was right and what was wrong. I felt responsible for protecting them and only wanted what was best for the church. Many times, I lay awake in bed, praying for wisdom and God's protective hand to cover us. *God is not the author of confusion, but of peace, as in all churches of the saints* (1 Corinthians 14:33).

It became clear that some of the former Amish wanted to go out and try other churches. Letting them go was agonizing for me, but when my own marriage and family life began to struggle, I knew I had to put things in God's hand and move on. I'd hoped to establish leadership in the church, but I made the mistake of trying to put together a doctrinal statement and church bylaws, which was viewed as too similar to the Amish ordinance letter with too much structure.

I was reminded of the Jews and Gentiles who were placing their faith in Jesus Christ during the early church. The Jews came out of a long legalistic background, while the Gentiles came from a background of idol worship and loose living. Suddenly, two complete opposites found themselves attending the same church. In the book of Ephesians, the apostle Paul explains how God brought the Jew and Gentile together through Christ. The same could be said for the Amish and English believers.

> *For he* [Christ] *is our peace, who hath made both one, and hath broken down the middle wall of partition between us; Having abolished in his flesh the enmity, even the law of commandments contained in ordinances; for to make in himself of twain one new man, so making peace; And that he might reconcile both unto God in one body by the cross, having slain the enmity thereby.* (Ephesians 2:14-16)

Understanding the book of Ephesians has often helped me see through a lens that tells me it can be healthy for two peoples to come together. Separation is unhealthy, so I don't recommend starting a former-Amish church. They bring all their pain and frustrations into that setting, so they need good, solid Bible-believing English people to help them with their anguish and difficulties.

When I first started with this ministry, I thought, *We're going* to pull a ton of former Amish into my home church. Instead, I find 90 percent of them start in our church and end up at other churches. As a result, they are in all kinds of churches in our area. At first I felt rejected; I thought we'd worship together, but that's not what God wants. Yes, Lord, these former Amish need to go to other churches and in this way influence each other in positive ways.

> For there is no difference between the Jew and the Greek [Amish and non-Amish]: for the same Lord over all is rich unto all that call upon him. For whosoever shall call upon the name of the Lord shall be saved. (Romans 10:12-13)

Chapter 19

MAP Outreach

For the past thirty years, Esther and I have taken adult individuals and families who have left the Amish into our home. Sometimes they were placed by court order. In spite of challenges along the way, we have always enjoyed this part of the ministry. We find great joy in helping young adults make something of themselves.

We have cried, mourned, and laughed with one another. We've endured many sleepless nights as we prayed earnestly for God to move in hearts and lives. We've had to deal with alcohol, drugs, sex, cursing, rebellion, and the law. We had to deal with parents who were angry at us because we gave their adult child a home. Some stole money and possessions from us, invited strangers into our home, and mocked us before others. Over the course of thirty years, however, we have witnessed the power and transformation of God's hand and have seen many young folks get saved, follow the Lord in baptism, and join a local church where they are now serving God and others.

Now that we have reached our fiftieth birthdays, Esther and I are ready to expand the outreach and invite others to participate in this relocation ministry for former Amish. With great excitement we have moved forward with a housing and counseling ministry known as New Beginnings.

Disappointed Amish parents have blamed us for pulling their children out of the Amish community, but we have never gone after anyone personally. If they land on our doorstep, we help in any way we can. It makes no difference if the individual is Amish or former Amish, because only culture and personal preferences divide the two groups.

Even as a young Amish boy, I had a desire to write in the Amish Budget or some other publications by the Amish. In 2007 my yearning became a reality. With some financial help from a church in Shinglehouse, Pennsylvania, we mailed our first 2,500 copies of the *Amish Voice* to various settlements in Ohio. Since then, we have not missed a single mailing. The sixteen-page publication now goes out to 8,000 Amish households every other month. Individuals and churches who have a heart for the Amish and their spiritual well-being pay for the printing and postage.

The purpose of the *Amish Voice* does not in any way try to lead people away from the Amish culture, nor is it used as a weapon to point out false teachings. Our main desire and goal is to share the gospel of Jesus Christ – to encourage, challenge, and educate our people spiritually.

Every household owns several Bibles, the *Martyr's Mirror*, a prayer book, and hymnbook. All four of these books are written in High German. Sadly, German is the least understood of their three languages, so many have a hard time understanding what they read. Instead, they trust their church leaders, traditions, heritage, and culture to prepare them for eternity.

In 2015, an Old Order Amish couple in northern Indiana wrote the following letter and distributed it to area ministers.

I believe it speaks for many who are searching for the truth or have already had their eyes opened to salvation.

> We write to you today concerning an issue in our Amish churches. After praying and feeling God's guidance in this matter, we feel we must bring this subject to light.
>
> This is concerning the use of the German language in our churches today. We know this tradition (some would call it a heritage) has been passed down from generation to generation from our forefathers, but what is of the fact that most of our people no longer understand this language? We no longer use this language anywhere but in church.
>
> Our main language is Pennsylvania Dutch, but before we go to school, we must learn the English language, and we must speak this language if we are to have a job or any communication with the world around us. Why is it then that on Sundays we are clinging to this tradition of using the German language? Most of us know how to read this language either from attending the Amish school or from Deitsh School, but sadly we do not know the meaning of the words. How sad it is to sit in church on Sunday, feeling the need to praise God in song but not knowing what the song we sing means (we have Our Heritage Hope and Faith book and Hymns book which would be ok, but we cannot take these books to church with us).
>
> A lot of preachers today are making an effort to explain these Scriptures in our everyday language (although many do not), but we feel this is not enough; our young

adults and children understand close to nothing! Is it any wonder that many are choosing not to stay Amish? Let's take a look at what God says:

1 Corinthians 14:18-19: *I thank my God, I speak with tongues more than ye all: Yet in the church I had rather speak five words with my understanding, that by my voice I might teach others also, than ten thousand words in an unknown tongue.*

Mark 7:6-8: *He answered and said unto them, Well hath Esaias prophesied of you hypocrites, as it is written, This people honoureth me with their lips, but their heart is far from me. Howbeit in vain do they worship me, teaching for doctrines the commandments of men. For laying aside the commandment of God, ye hold the tradition of men, as the washing of pots and cups: and many other such like things ye do.*

Revelation 3:15-16: *I know thy works, that thou art neither cold nor hot: I would thou wert cold or hot. So then because thou art lukewarm, and neither cold nor hot, I will spue thee out of my mouth.*

We ask the question – If our churches were not lukewarm, would we not be content to sit and sing songs we do not know the meaning of? Would we be content to preach the Good News of Jesus in a language that most of us do not understand? We understand that our Amish heritage has many traditions that are worth holding on to, and we are thankful for these things. But we must ask ourselves when our traditions stand in the way of people hearing and understanding the gospel of

Jesus, is it worth it? I fear our children are paying the price.

A word of encouragement:

Philippians 1:9-11: *And this I pray, that your love may abound yet more and more in knowledge and in all judgment; That ye may approve things that are excellent; that ye may be sincere and without offence till the day of Christ; Being filled with the fruits of righteousness, which are by Jesus Christ, unto the glory and praise of God.*

In closing, for fear of being written as such, we feel we must clarify: we are not part of Revive Indiana, or a Bible study group or any organization of any kind. We are simply an Old Order Amish couple with a concern for our church.

Please pray and seek God's will on the matter.

Sincerely,
A concerned Brother and Sister

We have chosen to withhold our names for fear of being shunned by the people for speaking boldly what God has laid on our heart.

The *Amish Voice Conference Line* is a phone ministry that allows up to one thousand callers to join. Topics vary from Bible doctrines to family, marriage, and testimonies. We have had well-known and popular counselors and authors lead these discussions. We record and upload them to a phone server, so Amish people can continue to call in and listen afterwards.

The *Sermons by Phone* ministry works in a similar fashion. Every month, we upload six new sermons for people to dial in and listen to. Listeners are encouraged to leave a message and a phone number. Both ministries are continually advertised in the *Amish Voice*.

Some Amish send their children to public schools for various reasons. This is more common in communities such as Holmes County, Ohio, and northern Indiana. A few Amish homeschool their children. Yet, the vast majority of Amish send their children to a one-room schoolhouse, a right they gained after much conflict in the 1930s. The issue made its way to the Supreme Court, which, in its landmark decision Wisconsin vs. Yoder (1972), granted the Amish and other religious minorities the right to remove their children from schooling after eighth grade or fourteen years of age, whichever comes first.

An eighth-grade education works fine for individuals who choose to stay in the Amish culture; however, when one chooses to leave and join mainstream American culture, they are faced with many disadvantages unless they further their education. Therefore, MAP also offers local and long-distance GED programs.

Fewer than 50 percent enroll in a GED program. Mostly, they don't see the value in education and would rather work in construction where a GED is not needed. A few, mostly girls, have chosen to further their education beyond a GED by attending college for a degree in nursing or teaching. Others get their GED in order to homeschool their children, volunteer at the fire station, secure higher-paying factory positions, obtain airplane licenses, and a multitude of other reasons.

In 2013, a pastor friend of mine called to propose a conference for people who wanted to learn more about the Amish culture and beliefs.

He said, "Joe, God has already given me a name – Amish Awareness Conference."

Shortly thereafter, we had our very first Amish Awareness Conference in Savannah, Ohio. About 150 people from ten states traveled there for the event, and major radio stations, including VCY America, Family Radio, Moody Radio, and local newspapers learned about the event and asked for interviews, which led to more conferences in other states.

Each two- to three-day conference is designed to help non-Amish and former Amish learn better ways to connect, evangelize, and disciple Amish individuals who live in our own backyards. One of the highlights is when we set up panel discussions for former Amish and English individuals to learn from each other.

I personally like the conferences because they provide a platform for the former Amish, who are less educated, to get in front of people and share their testimonies and preach. To date, there haven't been any events without someone making a commitment to go into ministry.

The heart of every Amish Awareness Conference is outlined in my 140-page book, *Amish: Our Friends, But Are They Believers?* Appendix D shows the details of the conference.

Since the day God called me to this ministry, I have been amazed at the doors He opens. We speak in churches about thirty weekends out of the year, as well as to hospital staff, law enforcement, and colleges. We usually speak to the outside world because they want to know how to communicate with the Amish. Doctors, nurses, and healthcare officials often question why the Amish churches don't allow their members to have medical insurance, or why they refuse to be transferred by life flight. I explain that many believe Satan lives and rules the space between heaven and earth. This is based on Ephesians 2:2 which says, *according to the prince of the power of the air, the spirit that now worketh in the children of disobedience.* Therefore, they don't want to enter Satan's kingdom.

While at the hospital, some Amish women refuse to remove their head covering. Sometimes, doctors are unable to send their Amish patients home as early as they wish because their sect forbids indoor bathroom facilities, which means they would have to be able to get up and walk to an outhouse.

Not everyone likes MAP Ministry. We have been threatened physically, and on three different occasions, non-Amish individuals have presented themselves as attorneys and threatened to file lawsuits against us. One person from the state of New York, who claimed to be an attorney, created a website. His goal was to turn people against us and shut the ministry down.

At other times, people stood up in the middle of our church presentations and argued that we were attacking the Amish and wondered why their pastor allowed us to come in.

One time a guy interrupted, "The Amish may not be born again, but at least they are Christians."

I've learned the best way to handle these situations is to go back and focus on the Amish culture. Most of the books and documentaries available to us today picture the culture, which is what we all like so much about the Amish. But then I'd continue my presentation by saying, we must separate the fascinating and beautiful culture from their religious beliefs.

Currently, MAP is preparing to build a 6,000-square-foot bulk food store called Beyond Measure Market. The store will be next to the MAP office building and New Beginnings counseling and housing ministries. Beyond Measure Market will serve as a place for young girls to get retail and customer experience while they live at New Beginnings and wait for their birth records, Social Security numbers, and GED certificates. The market will also serve as a way for us to pay for the housing and counseling expenses.

Someday we hope to have our own Bible school for young adults to get a greater understanding of God's work and ministry. With some help and proper training, more of my own people might go into ministry and be used of God. The Bible school will only offer biblical training and hands-on ministry opportunities. The goal is to spend as much time in practical ministry as sitting in a classroom. This huge project will require a lot of people's prayer support and funds.

God is using MAP, not only to reach out to the Amish, but to help educate non-Amish. MAP has been on ABC, PBS (*American Experience*), History Channel (*Seven Deadly Sins*), and National Geographic (*Amish Out of Order series*). MAP ministry has been on many radio stations, and has showed up in magazine articles, novels, and school textbooks.

Sometimes, I feel the distant rumble and awakening of another great revival coming to America. And when it does, this revival will come from within the Anabaptist communities. They are more zealous than any other people culture I know. The world has their eyes on the Amish, and many stand in amazement and wonder.

Chapter 20

Struggles With Authority

I still go as much as possible to our home church, where my brother Johnny teaches a former-Amish Sunday school class, and we have weekly Bible studies and prayer meetings at our house. During the summer, we have worship nights and play games to give young people things to do to help them stay off drugs and alcohol. My brothers William and Perry own construction businesses and have employed many young men. However, some of the former Amish have had to learn lessons the hard way by doing jail time or prison time. We've also seen some go on welfare. I guess it's like any other culture; you see it all.

Unfortunately, many former Amish struggle with authority. I have no doubt that much of the struggle comes from feeling forced to live under rules that don't make sense. The truth is, many families are large and life is always busy. Throw a bunch of man-made rules in the mix with little to no affection and a lack of proper training, and children rebel against their parents and all other authority.

Also, for the most part, these young people who come from the Amish culture have been taught to see themselves as above the law; this causes many to rebel against police authority. It doesn't take long for adults to see that rebelling against cops and judges doesn't work.

One young man, who lived with us for the second time around, was knocked to the ground one night and ended up with severe pavement burns when he tried to run from the highway patrol on a busy, six-lane highway in Columbus, Ohio. His cheekbones and face were so badly bruised I reported it to our local sheriff's department and had them come out to look at his face.

They made it clear, "Don't ever run away from cops and never get out of your car!"

Today, this same man lives in our home with a GPS bracelet on his ankle. He got caught for having a loaded gun on him and drugs in his car. He and I meet weekly to work on his finances and do a Bible study. I believe he will pull through and make something of himself, but like so many others, he had to be thrown in jail a few times and pay thousands of unnecessary dollars to cover the attorney's fees, court costs, and fines before he finally started to wise up.

I've met with our local judge and numerous attorneys behind closed doors and had police in my home asking in desperation, "How do we help them? They are very rebellious."

My only answer is, "There's not much you can do but let them learn the hard way."

I'll never forget the time five young boys got very irritated with me. They were sending me threatening text messages and spreading all kinds of false accusations on Facebook about me and the ministry. One day I phoned one of the boys and said, "Let's get together and handle this like men. You round up the other four, and I'll meet you at your house."

I walked in and found the living room corner stacked several feet high with empty beer cans. They were all cocked, loaded, and ready to put me in my place.

I said, "Before we get started, let me pray and ask God to lead us."

While I prayed, I could hear silent mocking going on. Then one after the other, they shared things they felt I did wrong. At one point, Bill got up and went upstairs. When he returned, he laid a loaded revolver between him and me. I refused to flinch.

Most of what came out of the five boys was pain and anger from the past. I did not take their accusations personally, but tried my best to understand and respond in love. In the end, everybody felt good, and I went home thanking God that I could serve Him and a few young men who will most likely grow up and become good citizens of our great country.

We have an area downstairs in our home that has been turned into a three-bedroom apartment. Several years ago, Malinda showed up at our ministry from another state, but soon got caught for stealing from our local Walmart and landed in jail for a while. Later, we learned Malinda was hiding a Mexican man in the apartment. Because Mexican and former-Amish both feel like outsiders in the American culture, they seem to connect and tend to gravitate toward one another. One night, I was sure the Mexican had snuck into our apartment again, so I pushed a couch up against the door that separated our area from the apartment. When I caught him in the apartment again and realized Malinda was not going to follow our signed live-in agreement, I called the police and both Malinda and the Mexican were asked to leave.

Before Malinda left the Amish, she had written:

In this life of hardships and sufferings, I have to wonder where is God through it all? Without God, life is impossible, but with Him it is hard. Satan tries to make life look unbearable. Into my life comes darkness like a thief in the night, robbing the light of my life. Praying is in vain.

Every way I turn there is darkness, absolutely no light.

I cry out for mercy, but this is what I hear, "You are a sinner doomed to hell, you are worthless, not fit to live. I have you where I want you, in the pit of darkness, the next thing to hell."

There is no way out; if there is, I cannot see it. The light is gone. Oh God have mercy on me.

"Oh but he does not hear," Satan says.

Life is rough and it will continue to be so. I am torn up inside, but nobody can see that.

The pain is numbing, especially when nobody cares. I want to leave it all but don't know how.

All of my days I have never felt loved. I feel like a rag all wrung out and worn.

After much debate, I reach my decision, pain is eating me alive. Life isn't worth living.

Hell can't be worse, I hear myself think. God forgive me, but it is too late.

With my finger on the trigger, I squeeze, shut my eyes, with one more cry,

"God, please don't let me do this!"

I held my breath for a few seconds, my arms went slack. "Thank you Lord," I said.

In another situation, two girls secretly invited a man to stay with them in our apartment. He was fresh out of prison and needed a place to live. After hiding in our apartment downstairs for two weeks, his mom called us one day and said, "Do you know my son is living in your house? He has a wife and two children and needs to come back to them."

I mentioned this earlier, but it bears repeating. I'm aware that some of what I share in this book will offend some Amish and former Amish, so I want to be really clear about something. According to Ohio State University, there are about forty different subcultures of Amish. Many who come to us are from the more conservative sects. The more liberal, open-minded Amish usually already have their Social Security numbers and better hygiene habits, and they transition into the English culture with greater ease. They are also less rebellious, have a higher standard of manners, and don't resort to drugs and alcohol as often. This proves once again that man-made rules and legalism do not work, and they don't turn a person into a Christian. *The letter* [law] *killeth, but the spirit giveth life* (2 Corinthians 3:6b).

This verse is simply pointing out that the letter (old covenant) was a list of written words, a written document, a set of laws that God required His people to follow and obey. Consider that the law was external; it sat outside man like a piece of clothing and insisted that man surrender himself to the rule and obey it.

Did it work? No! Therefore, God brought us a new and better covenant (Hebrews 8:6). The law, under the old covenant, constantly pointed its finger in people's noses and cried guilty, guilty, guilty! Guilt brings on condemnation, and condemnation results in depression and rebellion against authority.

The new covenant is entirely different. It is internal, within man – a personal relationship with God that is created by God Himself. When a person is born again, God places His Spirit in the heart of the person, and the person becomes a Spirit-filled,

Spirit-led person. *For the law was given by Moses, but **grace and truth** came by Jesus Christ* (John 1:17, emphasis added).

As Jesus preached throughout Judea and Samaria, He told the woman at the well, *The hour cometh, and now is, when the true worshippers shall worship the Father in **spirit and in truth**: for the Father seeketh such to worship him. God is a Spirit: and they that worship him must worship him in **spirit and in truth*** (John 4:23-24, emphasis added).

We have helped many a son and daughter in our ministry who've gone through much of what I did. In most cases, the parents and children lost their connection early in the child's life, and it hurts when parents deny their responsibility and accuse our ministry and others for taking their children away. Compared to the English culture, Amish parents often lack the resources and helps we have taken for granted. A century ago, their style of raising a family may have worked, but times have changed and will continue to change.

As Esther and I raised our own family, we learned something from James Dobson which helped us as parents. He said that as our children mature, they naturally want to pull away from us even though we naturally want to hold on. If we can let them go, they will grow into the adults that God wants them to be. Colossians 3:21 says, *Fathers, provoke not your children to anger, lest they be discouraged.* Parents need to be careful in this regard.

Two things will provoke a child:

1. Failing to accept the fact that things do change. Time and generations change. Parents need to be alert to the changes between generations and allow the child to be a part of his or her own generation instead of trying to conform the child to the parent's childhood generation.

2. Over-controlling a child will also provoke a child to
   wrath. Over-control ranges all the way from stern
   restriction and discipline to child abuse, which
   will either stifle the growth of a child or stir him
   to react and rebel.

The point is this: there must be a balance between family life
and the child's community life. The child should be allowed to
do his own thing sometimes and should be required to share
with the family at other times. As he grows older, he should
be allowed to break away more and more to prepare him for
when he will step out into the world on his own.

In most Amish families, the father does not have a lot of
time to spend with the children, so often instead of loving and
caring for them, they just discipline them and force them back
into the mold and keep them there. That turns the son against
the father, and the more the son turns against this rigid life, the
more the father tries to force him into the mold, which leads
to more problems.

In my case, I left to find someone to fill that hole. I found
Eli and Levi, and drugs and alcohol. The void led me down the
path of stealing money from Amish homes, rebelling against
every authority that stood in the way, lusting after women, and
falling into sexual sins. By the grace of God, I did not end up
in prison like some others have.

My experience with a young man named Atlee offers the
perfect illustration of how many Amish fathers interact with
their sons. Atlee was eighteen when he left the Amish and came
to our doorstep, asking if he could move in with us. When his
dad came to visit him for the first time, he ran and hid. He
didn't want to see his father.

I invited the father, Davie, into our home and for the next

hour we discussed his relationship with Atlee. Davie and I had attended school together, so I knew him very well.

I asked, "Davie, how do you show love to your son, Atlee? Do you ever let him know you appreciate the work he does on the farm? Do you ever sit down with your son and encourage him, make him feel needed and important? That's what he is trying to figure out."

Davie nodded slowly. "Yes, I've done that."

"How did you do that?" I asked.

"Well, I try to remember to tell him good night before he goes to bed."

Davie's short answer came from a sincere father who I believe loved his son very much. Otherwise, he would not have been sitting in my living room asking to see him. The sad truth is he probably didn't know how to show real love to his son. How could he if it was never shown or taught by the previous generation?

I went back to where Atlee was hiding, and I asked him, "Have you ever gotten a hug from your father?"

"No, never."

"Has he ever told you that he loves you?"

"No, never."

"Has he ever patted you on the back and said good job, son?"

"No, never."

I knew exactly how he felt and went over and hugged him. I said, "Around here we give each other hugs. It's something we all need."

Unfortunately, most Amish don't hug. They aren't affectionate. It's more of a get-up-early, work-hard-all-day, come-in-late-at-night, and-go-to-bed lifestyle with little appreciation verbalized. Many of the young people who come to us are tired of working so hard with little or no appreciation. When they leave the Amish, you just have to let them sort through it in their own time.

I always tell myself and others, "Get your eyes off the now and look out five years. Until then, just love on them, even when it is very hard to do."

The most challenging, and also most important, thing is to believe in your teenage child and make him or her feel special and valued. Sometimes you need to love them enough to let them make decisions, even if you see it's a mistake. They will learn from their mistakes and that will help them grow into functioning adults who know how to make wise choices.

———————

Some saved Amish groups are preaching the gospel in their churches. Some time ago, I sat between two Amish men in a barn, and before us was a workbench nailed to the wall with a portable DVD player on it. The man on my left was born again and on fire for the Lord, but the man on my right was an alcoholic. His marriage and family were about to fall apart; he was buried in pornography and suffered from horrible money problems. The three of us sat watching a DVD on how to put your marriage back together.

The saved man said, "In my church people get saved, but we keep the lifestyle. The lifestyle is not wrong, but trusting in it to get you to heaven is wrong."

I fully agreed and thanked God for the man's testimony.

As much as I'm thankful for those who are preaching the gospel and seeing people surrender their lives to Christ, I still have a question. Why is it that a non-Amish person, who wants to join the group and become a member of the church has to first renounce and forsake his previous lifestyle, get re-baptized into the Amish church, conform to Amish-style clothing patterns, use horse and buggy for transportation, switch from electricity to gas-powered lighting, learn the German language, and submit to other rules?

On the other hand, if an Amish person asked to join our church, we would only require two things. (1) When did you surrender your life to Jesus Christ? And, (2) have you followed the Lord in baptism? Beyond that, we wouldn't mind at all if they chose a type of transportation that was different than ours. We wouldn't mind if they chose to wear Amish clothes or use gas-powered lights instead of electric and farm with horse-drawn farm equipment. From my perspective, these things are all secondary issues, personal preferences, and should never be enforced by the leadership of the church.

The endless rules create the struggle that the young people have with the Amish culture, and ultimately with authority in general.

Chapter 21

Difficulties and Blessings

Without a doubt in my mind, God called Esther and me into the ministry to the Amish and former Amish. Even though ministry has sometimes been difficult and caused us many tears and sleepless nights, we don't doubt that we are in the center of God's will. Just like the apostle Paul and others who ministered before us, we are servants of Christ and have been called to meet the desperate needs of the world and reach men with the glorious news that Christ will save them from an eternal hell and give them life that lasts forever. Every day people around us are being thrust into eternity to face Almighty God. *Therefore, my beloved brethren, be ye stedfast, unmoveable, always abounding in the work of the Lord, forasmuch as ye know that your labour is not in vain in the Lord* (1 Corinthians 15:58).

The Amish people are just like us and the rest of the world. Some are loving, generous, kind, and understanding. Others are bitter, hateful, and angry. Some live secret lives of sin and shame. Some are born again and on fire for the Lord, while the rest are steeped in darkness and do not understand salvation.

I once talked to an Amish man, Willard, who grew up in a

Schwartzentruber sect in Holmes County, Ohio. In his young adult life, he had left the Schwartzentruber sect for a different Amish group. When he left the Schwartzentruber church, he was excommunicated and shunned. The New Order Amish church received Willard into membership. When the lot fell on Willard and he became a preacher in the new church, his sister – still part of the Schwartzentruber church – almost went out of her mind.

"Why would God choose my brother to preach when he has been turned over to Satan?" she exclaimed to her family.

After a few years, the church where Willard attended needed a bishop. Again, the congregation got together and cast lots; again it fell on Willard. When the sister found out what happened, she completely lost it.

When Bishop Willard shared the story with me, he said, "You know, Joe, you can get much further by pounding your forehead against the fence post all day than you can talking to some Amish people. At least after a day of pounding the post, you get to walk away with a big welt on your forehead, which is far more than you get when talking to some Amish about the one true gospel."

With that in mind, let me share how we have been yelled at and chased out of Amish homes for opening up about the gospel. The Amish have come to our home and threatened to hurt us physically. Some have called our office and cursed us, while others have written letters in anger.

In one particular situation, we spoke at a church in Shinglehouse, Pennsylvania. Afterward, an older couple, Ernie and Joyce, approached us and shared how they had been actively witnessing to an Amish family in their area for over twenty years.

"Would you and Esther consider going with us and visiting them?" they asked.

The next day the four of us piled into their van and drove to see their Amish friends. We were all welcomed into their home and began to visit. This family did not know Esther and me, but about thirty minutes into our conversation, I began to share my salvation testimony.

The father jumped to his feet and yelled, "Get out! Get out! Get out of my house now!"

Within sixty seconds we were out in the van. As Ernie was preparing to back out of the driveway, the door opened up, and the father yelled to Ernie and Joyce, "Don't you dare take Joe and Esther to visit my married sons and daughters."

My Father

For many years, Esther and I prayed for all our family members by name and fasted one day a week with great desire that God would open their hearts to salvation. When our children, Jonathan and Rachel, got old enough to pray, they joined us and prayed earnestly that God would save Grandpa, Grandma, and all their uncles and aunts.

I remember the first time I shared the salvation message with my dad. He had sent word that he would be coming to visit at our house. I was sure God was answering our prayers and that my dad would come to an understanding of biblical salvation. My brother William came to our house, and we prayed over every spot we thought he might walk. We prayed over the entire length of the driveway, the telephone pole where he would be tying his horse, and the couch he'd sit on. When Dad finally arrived, we invited him into the house and sat together in the living room.

The first few hours were spent talking about family back home and his overwhelming concern for us who were living in the world. Not only was he worried that Esther and I would end in divorce but also that our children would end up in spiritual confusion and turn their backs on God and the local church. He said it with such confidence and surety that it brought fear to my heart. Along the way, he reminded me that he had been around for a lot longer than me, and he had seen it happen multiple times to others who left the Amish church.

It was very hard for me to know how to start, but at about midnight, I pulled my Bible out and began to share God's plan of salvation with him. It was now my turn to share the concerns I had for him and the rest of the family. He sat back and listened in complete silence as I covered one Scripture passage after another.

"Dad, according to God's Word, salvation is not what we do for God, but rather what God has done for us."

I shared my entire testimony of how I had called upon the name of the Lord and was born again on July 28, 1985. When I got to the end of my study, I walked over, knelt down before him, and begged him to fully surrender his life to Jesus Christ and believe in his heart that Jesus alone could save him from his sins and hell.

As I begged and pleaded with him, my dad just stared straight ahead and did not say a word. Finally, he stood up, reached for his hat, and walked out through the living room into the dining and kitchen area. I realized he was going to leave and not say a word. I jumped up and ran after him.

As he was going through the outside door, I yelled, "Dad, are you not going to respond at all?"

He stopped and looked straight at me. All he said was, "Whatever you do, Joe, please don't ever enlist in the military."

I believe Dad thought all English people join the military or at least believe in it. I also believe he felt that when he served a year of prison for refusing to participate in the Vietnam War, he was suffering persecution right along with our Anabaptist forefathers and, in a sense, earning his rights to salvation.

As my dad drove into the night, I did not know if we would ever see each other again. His concerns for me were just as real as my concerns for him. *Why,* I wondered, *did life have to be so complicated?*

The Reunion

For twenty years we heard very little from my family except for a few letters. One after the other, my brothers and sisters got married, but we were never informed or invited. Knowing that we only lived fifteen miles away made it even harder.

Then out of the blue, two of my married sisters decided to have a family reunion and include our family and my three brothers and their families who'd left the Amish. Everything was kept hush-hush. They did not want their community to find out, nor did they want everybody in the Keim family to know, fearing some would refuse to show for the reunion if they knew we were invited.

To keep tension to a minimum, my married sisters, Saloma and Ella, asked us to park our cars about a mile away at an English neighbor's farm. Saloma and Ella, who had done all the planning, lived across the field from each other. So, we parked the cars and walked to Ella's house and put on the Amish clothes they had laid out for us to wear. From there, we walked across the field to Saloma's house, where most of our Amish families had already gathered for the reunion.

Dad and Mom now had ninety grandchildren, and they were all there. I hadn't seen some of my siblings for twenty years. When the time came to eat, we all gathered in the pole barn. One table was set up for Amish families and another for former Amish. By church standards, we were not allowed to fill our plate from the same container.

I spotted Dad with gray hair; Mom too. For the first time in twenty years, we were all together. They enjoyed it as much as we did. We talked about our daily lives, listened to children's laughter, and played softball. At the end of the day though, we walked back into our world, and they stayed in theirs. Later we found out that Mom and Dad were disciplined by the church for accepting us in. That upset me, but I realized there was very little anyone could do.

Reconciliation

Soon after that reunion, I felt a great need to go and get some personal counseling. I realized that even though I was in the ministry and had dealt with all kinds of young people, my past often got in the way of ministry. Esther and I decided to go to North Carolina to get away from everyone who knew us in the ministry. I didn't want anyone to know I needed help, and felt somewhat embarrassed. We took five full days of counseling and about the fourth day I realized I still had a lot of stored-up anger toward my father that went way back to my childhood. On day five I had a breakthrough and handed everything over to the Lord. Five days of intense counseling left me emotionally and mentally drained, but I also felt like a great heaviness had left me when I released all the anger toward my father.

On the way home, I said, "I can't change Dad, but I need to go and apologize to him for everything I've done to hurt him." My brother William agreed to go with me.

My parents had left the Amish in Ohio and moved to Pennsylvania to another community. They'd been there five years, but I hadn't been there yet. On August 5, 2011, William and I headed east toward Ulysses, Pennsylvania. While many people prayed, we prepared ourselves for rejection. By the time we found Dad and Mom's place, way out in the middle of nowhere, it was 9:00 p.m. and completely dark.

We drove in the driveway and spotted what looked like a small light moving to and fro in the pitch-black darkness.

Mom was out doing chores with a headlamp strapped to her forehead, but she had no idea who we were. When we got close enough, she turned her little head-lamp toward our faces and studied us for what seemed like forever.

Suddenly, she exclaimed, "Joe? Is that you, Joe? And William?"

"Yes, it's us," not knowing for sure what to expect.

Would they let us in the house or not? Much to our relief, Dad came along and invited us into the house. That night we talked and talked and talked.

At about 2:00 a.m., Dad said, "Why don't you just stay here for the night?"

We both responded, "Yes, we would love to."

When we awoke the next morning, the smell of Mom's cooking came up through the registers in the floor. When we came downstairs, we noticed that two tables were set. Dad motioned for us to sit at our table, while they sat at theirs.

After a silent prayer, Mom said, "OK boys, dive in and eat. There's plenty."

As we chowed away on Mom's home-cooked breakfast that morning, I couldn't think of any other place on earth I'd rather be.

After breakfast, I shared how much I regretted the pain and embarrassment I had brought on our family during my teenage years. I also shared how Esther and I had traveled to North Carolina a few months earlier and gone through five days of counseling.

Dad in turn shared what it was like for him during those times I left the Amish. He could hardly talk through his tears, and like me, he had an immense amount of pain stored up and pushed back over a twenty-five-year period. He shared many regrets as a father and wished he could go back and do some things over in life.

Dad told us what it was like for him the night he was hiding in the weeds, while Esther and I waited for our ride at the dark country crossroad.

"Joe, when you jumped on the back of Chuck's truck and drove away, in spite of my crying out to you, I sank to a new low in my life."

He went on to describe what it was like when he came to visit me in Mount Vernon, Ohio, a few days later.

"I hired a taxi driver to come and see you, hoping I could get you to come home with me. When we got to the house where you were staying, Chuck came out and told me to leave. He said, 'Joe does not want to talk.' So I waited on the doorstep until four o'clock in the morning. Again, Chuck came out and was very angry with me. He ordered me to leave or he would call the police.

"At that point, I gathered myself together, got in the car, and headed home. The driver played "Hold Fast to the Right" in his tape player – six times through. This gave me the strength I so desperately needed to get through the pain of losing my oldest son."

When Dad got done telling the story, he said, "If you don't mind, I'd like to get my songbook and sing "Hold Fast to the Right" together."

As you can imagine, the tears were unstoppable for all of us as we sang about kneeling by our mother's side and receiving her parting advice. We sang about being tried by the world with temptations and trials. And we sang about confiding in the Savior and holding fast to the right.

When we finished, I asked Dad and Mom and my brother William, "Could we just go to God and give Him all our pain?" It was too much for us to handle on our own.

Mom responded, "We better let Dad pray."

I worried that Dad would pray out of his German prayer book, but instead, we all went down on our knees, and he prayed in Pennsylvania Dutch. As we prayed together on the living room floor, he wept aloud.

Finally, I couldn't hold on any longer. I got up, walked over to Dad, and asked if I could hold him in my arms. He stood to his feet, and we both threw our arms around each other. For the next ten minutes, we both wept bitterly and uncontrollably. As we held on to each other, our shirts became soaked with tears. It was as if twenty-five years of regrets, confusion, mis-understandings, and turmoil burst out from the deepest parts of our beings. In the end, we asked each other for forgiveness for the many times we hurt each other.

My love for Dad and Mom cannot be explained in words. I didn't want our time to end, but we had our own families and another world we lived in.

Dad and Mom didn't want us to leave either. As we stood and looked in each other's eyes, we wondered how we could possibly separate after such an emotional time.

Then William said, "I just have one question. If you died right now, do you have assurance that you're going to heaven?"

As much as we would have liked to hear, "Yes, we are born again," or "Yes, we are confident of our salvation," we didn't hear either. In the end, we had to let salvation go and put our parents back in God's hands.

We tried to leave seven times that morning, but each time something came up, and we returned and talked more. The last three times we were already heading toward our vehicle. Mom had loaded our car with all kinds of fruits, vegetables, and family keepsakes. As we pulled out, they yelled, "Please tell your wives and children we love them."

Dalton and Dad

Two years later, tragedy struck. My brother William and his wife, Jenica, had purchased a new home. Their son Dalton was two years old and playing in the kitchen while Jenica was busy cooking a wild turkey in boiling hot water. Little Dalton grabbed the oven door handle and somehow pulled the kitchen range forward, and all the boiling water dumped out on his little body. Within twenty-four hours, this beautiful child was dead.

When Dalton died, we wondered if our Amish family would come to the funeral. The funeral service was to be held in our home church. Years earlier my dad had made a vow that he would never step foot in our church building.

On the day of the funeral we got up to face our difficult day, not knowing if Mom and Dad and the rest of our Amish family would be there. At about 8:00 a.m., William called and said, "Dad just called and said he and Mom have been traveling most of the night. They plan to be at the funeral, but with one condition: 'That Joe does not get up and say anything from the pulpit.'"

"Really, William! You can't be serious," I said.

"Yes, Dad made it clear, 'If we come in there and Joe gets up and says anything at all, we'll have to get up and leave.'"

I couldn't believe what I was hearing, and it didn't make sense that my dad could control me on my own turf. If it was the other way around, I would have understood.

Finally, I said, "Okay, William, it hurts very deeply, but I want our dad and mom to be at the funeral more than I want to get up and speak from the pulpit."

I called my pastor quickly and said, "Please remove me from the schedule."

Our home church, where we have attended since the day we left the Amish in 1987, is big enough for four hundred people, and on the day of the funeral, it was filled except for two spots on the very front pew. We had kept those two spots open for Mom and Dad.

It was almost jaw dropping as we watched my seventy-year-old dad and mom walk in the back door. Every eye trained on them. Everyone knew our story. The usher brought them all the way down the aisle and sat them in the front pew. I couldn't help but wonder if Dad remembered his vow to never set foot in our church building.

My pastor got up and preached a message like it was his last. "You are either born again, or you are still lost and searching! You're either on your way to heaven or on the road that leads to hell. It is that simple – if you will believe and receive God's gift, He will give you everlasting life. God tells us in Romans: *For there is no difference between the Jew and the Greek: for the same Lord over all is rich unto all that call upon him. For whosoever shall call upon the name of the Lord shall be saved* (Romans 10:12-13). If you are sitting here today, and the Holy Spirit is speaking to your heart, I'm going to ask you to call upon the name of the Lord for salvation."

Moments later, Pastor John asked, "With heads bowed and eyes closed, how many of you prayed and asked the Lord to save you?" Many hands went up, and the pastor thanked each one for being honest.

As I walked past the coffin one last time and shook hands with my brother William, he totally lost control. With tears spilling down his face, he pulled me in.

"I now know why Dalton died," he said. "When the pastor asked people who prayed for salvation to lift their hands, I couldn't help but look up. Dad and Mom both raised their hands."

For the next few minutes, we both wept, praised the Lord out loud, and began to realize the purpose of our sweet little Dalton and his early departure. It made it easier for us to let go.

Where has my relationship gone with Dad and Mom since the funeral? Let me just say, it may have taken thirty long years to break down the thick walls, but I feel very comfortable jumping in the car and visiting my parents. Obviously, they live in the Amish world, and I live in the English world. A feeling of separation will always be there, but we are both learning to live with the differences.

When Dad and Mom celebrated their 50th anniversary last October, we were all invited to join our Amish family for the special event. Dad and Mom were the center of attention, and we loved on them. Yes, we still had to eat at separate tables, but we refused to let that bother us. We had so much fun that day and felt very much a part of the English/Amish/Jewish family that we are.

Chapter 22

In God's Eyes

In God's eyes, there is no difference between Amish and non-Amish people. No difference in lifestyles, cultures, and church denominations. No difference between Anabaptists and Protestants. No difference between who our forefathers were and today's generation. These labels are all man-made and have divided us for too long. *All we like sheep have gone astray; we have turned everyone to his own way* (Isaiah 53:6a).

When the Scripture says **all** *we like sheep have gone astray,* it means ALL. Not one single culture, church denomination, man, woman, or child is exempt. We have all gone our own way. The prophet Isaiah continues to write, *But we are **all** as an unclean thing, and **all** our righteousnesses are as filthy rags* (Isaiah 64:6a, emphasis added). What we do on our own to obtain right standing with the Lord is completely insufficient. The Bible can be trusted when it says, *For he hath made him to be sin for us, who knew no sin; that we might be made the righteousness of God in him* (2 Corinthians 5:21).

The Law of Moses was needed to bring mankind to an understanding of his own sinfulness and need for Jesus Christ.

There's no such thing as many doorways into heaven. It's not the Amish way, the Baptist way, the charismatic way, or the Pentecostal way. It's the Jesus way.

Just suppose four of us died and went to heaven. One day, while sitting together in a circle, I asked, "How did the three of you get here?"

The first one replied, "I got here because my forefathers came out of the Great Awakening in 1734."

The second man replied, "I'm here because my forefathers came out of Welsh Revival in 1905."

Not to be outdone, the third one replied, "I got all of you beat. I'm here because my forefathers were the Anabaptists."

What a pathetic conversation that would be! The truth is, if we could go back to each one of those persecuted forefathers and seek advice from them, they would all say, "God forbid that you look to us. We were just sinful human beings in desperate need of a Savior." I have no doubt they would all say, "Do what we all did. Set your eyes on Jesus Christ."

Jesus is the answer to all the pride, prejudice, bitterness, hatred, and disunity in our world. The ground at the foot of the cross is level. No person is accepted for any other reason than faith in Jesus Christ and His finished work on the cross.

> *Neither is there salvation in any other: for there is none other name under heaven given among men, whereby we must be saved.* (Acts 4:12)

When are we going to start acting like Spirit-filled children of God – caring more about others than ourselves, our traditions, our denominations? How much longer before we fall on our faces before God and cry out for forgiveness? Is severe persecution the only tool God has left to bring us to our knees?

From the beginning of our ministry, I've been burdened to come together and pray – not a time to fellowship, not a time for Bible study, but a prayer meeting. We get together for two hours every week to pray for lives to be changed. We pray for hundreds of young people who have come through the ministry. We pray for God to send an awakening. Some of those who prayed with us fourteen years ago are still coming. We pray for each other, too. We pray for fathers to lead, mothers to lead, and children to come to Christ.

One seventeen-year-old Amish boy showed up one night for the prayer meeting. He had cancer. His brother had already died from cancer, and the doctor said he only had a couple more weeks to live. He was so weak he could hardly sit in the chair. We laid hands on him and asked if it was God's will, that He would heal him. That boy is alive today. No cancer. He will tell you he got healed that night. He went back to the doctor who said, "I don't know where your cancer went."

Thank you for taking the time to read *My People, the Amish*. From the beginning, I prayed that God would use the story of my life to encourage you to never give up, regardless of your circumstances. James wrote: *For what is your life? It is even a vapour, that appeareth for a little time, and then vanisheth away.* (James 4:14b)

Just like a vapor that rises from a tea kettle, so our life appears and then is gone, vanished away. King Solomon had everything this world had to offer, and yet, in all his worldly splendor and glory, he cried out, *Then shall the dust return to the earth as it was: and the spirit shall return unto God who gave it. Vanity of vanities, saith the preacher, all is vanity* (Ecclesiastes 12:7-8). He knew he would soon be dust, and someone else would take over his kingdom and riches. He concluded, *Let us hear the conclusion of the whole matter: Fear God, and keep his commandments: for this is the whole duty of man* (Ecclesiastes 12:13).

Ah reader, if God has led you to these final words of mine, and you have not yet found your way to Him, let me point the way by sharing the cry of Jesus. He said, *"I am the way, the truth, and the life: no man cometh unto the Father, but by me"* (John 14:6).

The unlimited grace of God, through Jesus Christ, is drawing near to you and wants to replace your sin-stained heart with a new one. Listen to what He says: *A new heart also will I give you, and a new spirit will I put within you: and I will take away the stony heart out of your flesh, and I will give you an heart of flesh. And I will put my spirit within you* (Ezekiel 36:26-27a).

Will you accept the Lord's invitation? Go ahead. You can take a moment and talk with Him. He's right next to you, waiting.

I hope you said yes. If you did, Jesus promised, *He that heareth my word, and believeth on him that sent me, **hath** everlasting life, and **shall not** come into condemnation; but is **passed** from death unto life* (John 5:24, emphasis added).

Prayer

Father in heaven, I have sinned against You. I have strayed from You and gone after idols and man-made religion. I've done my own thing. I've lost my way. Have mercy on me, oh God, because of Your unfailing love. Because of Your great compassion, blot out the stain of my sins. Wash me clean from my guilt. Purify me from my sin. I recognize my rebellion. It haunts me day and night. You do not desire a sacrifice, or I would offer one. You do not want a burnt offering. The sacrifice you desire is a broken spirit. You will not reject a broken and repentant heart, oh God. (Based on Psalm 51)

Team Up with MAP

If you're interested, you have an opportunity to team up with MAP Ministry through prayer and giving. Our ministry is faith-based and only possible because of donors. If you want more information on how you can get involved, visit our website or feel free to contact us.

Contact Information

MAP Ministry
575 US Highway 250
P.O. Box 128
Savannah, OH 44874

Phone: (419) 962-1515
www.mapministry.org

Appendix A

My Perfect Father

By Rachel Keim

According to Webster's College Dictionary, the word *perfect* means "excellent or complete beyond practical or theoretical improvement." When Webster's College Dictionary created a definition for the word *perfect*, they were defining my father. There may be many good fathers present in the world, but none could outshine my father: my father is perfect. My father is a giving, considerate, and protective man, and he is my role model. My father exhibits the characteristics of perfection.

My father is giving. Winston Churchill once said, "We make a living by what we get, but we make a life by what we give." All of my life my father has gone against human nature and has put others above himself on a constant basis. I remember a time after my father went into full-time ministry that he did not get paid for three months. During that three-month period of no pay, my father continued to faithfully give his money to an organization that aided third-world countries. My father gave willingly even during difficult times. My father lives by Winston Churchill's words and gives, not only to his family, but also to those who are in need around him. My father has characterized his life by a giving heart.

My father is considerate of others. Although my dad believes that he is the "man of the house" and that he has the final say in all family matters, he is always willing to listen to everyone's viewpoint before making a decision. After genuinely listening to each person and making each individual feel as if his opinion is important, my father will earnestly try to make an agreeable decision. My father always strives for fairness.

My father is protective. As a child, I remember waking up once in the middle of the night, convinced that someone was breaking into the house. The first place I ran to for protection was my father. Within minutes of hearing my imaginative yet sincere tale, my father was out of bed and searching every room of the house until I felt confident that I was safe. This little act showed me that no matter how small the situation in life, my father will always be willing to do everything he can to protect me and my family.

My father is my role model. Every day I see traits in my father that I want to attain. When I was a little girl, I had made up my mind that I was going to marry my father. As I got older, I realized the heartbreaking fact that my fortunate mother was married to my father, and that my idea of marrying him would be impossible. Now, I only hope to marry a man one day who will be like my father and follow the model he has created.

Ten years ago, I sincerely believed with all of my heart that my father was perfect. Now that I am older, I realize that my father is not completely perfect, but I also realize that he strives for perfection every day. Because of his effort and the character traits he exhibits, my father is perfect in my eyes. I only hope that one day I can inherit some of his priceless qualities; after all, I'd like to be as close to perfect as possible.

Appendix B

Questions for David
Before Dating Rachel

By Joe Keim

Have you dated before?

Why are you attracted to Rachel?

Describe for me what you think dating is about.

How would you describe a good husband/leader in the home?

Tell me, how does a person get to heaven?

What is your strongest spiritual gift?

Share a weakness that you know you have.

How is your walk with the Lord (past and present)?

What areas of ministry have you been involved in?

What are three things, written in the Bible, that you feel very strong about?

Who do you look up to? Who's been your mentor?

What are your hobbies?

What is your relationship like with your family?

We have prayed for the following things:

- Rachel's and her man's purity all the way to marriage. (Comment on what purity means to you.)

- That her man would be a born-again Christian, raised in a godly home, and serving the Lord with all his heart.

- That her man would be a leader in the home (explain leading vs. pushing). Rachel cautioned, "Dad, this one might be a little intense. By all means, you can mention it (it is important). Hah! Just don't make too strong of a point of it for the poor guy!

Where do you want to be one year from now? Five years from now? Ten years from now?

How to end our conversation: "I am happy to give you permission to date my daughter." Rachel said, "Perfect! But remember, you don't *have* to give permission. I trust your judgment!"

Appendix C

Marriage Comments/ Questions for David

By Joe Keim

Our family has prayed thousands of times over many years that God would send Rachel a godly man – one who would protect her as well as lead her in the Lord's way. We do not want to sound controlling, nor do we want to hang on to Rachel for the rest of her life. The Bible says clearly in Matthew:

> *And he [Jesus] answered and said unto them, Have ye not read, that he [God] which made them at the beginning made them male and female, And said, For this cause shall a man leave father and mother, and shall cleave to his wife: and they twain shall be one flesh?* (Matthew 19:4-5)

Since the beginning of time, God meant for children to leave their parents and cleave only to their spouse. As parents, we are grateful and feel very blessed that God has allowed us to pour our hearts and lives into Rachel. Our goal from the beginning was to prepare her for the man that God would someday send her way. We may not always have measured up to what we should have or could have done, but one thing is for sure, we tried our very best.

Until Rachel left for college, we sat down on the couch with her every morning and asked God that He would protect her, fill her with His Holy Spirit, give her wisdom, and lead her in the right direction. It was also during those prayer times that we asked God to provide a born-again, godly husband for her – one who was raised in a home where they went to church and made God and family first and most important.

When Rachel was just a baby, we brought her before the church and made a commitment to bring her up in the nurture of the Lord. When she turned ten, we sat down with her and read through a series of books that explained how the Lord had made her in fear and wonder. It was also during those times that we shared what she should expect as she grew older – she would get married and have her own children. Later, at the age of sixteen, we invited eight godly men and women to come to our house to pray over Rachel. That same day, Rachel made a vow to stay sexually pure and follow the Lord all the days of her life.

Now that you and Rachel have been courting for two years, it's important that you know you are on our daily prayer list. Almost every weeknight for the past two years, Esther and I sat down together on the couch and prayed for the two of you.

It's been exciting to watch as God gave you and Rachel a desire to read book after book on healthy, godly marriages and families – you get ten stars for doing a GREAT job and leading the way. We are impressed by your knowledge of the Scriptures and the stand you have taken to stay sexually pure. Truly, the Lord has answered our prayers and done a great work!

Our family loves the Garwood family and considers all of you as dear friends and co-laborers in the Lord. We love the way you all have made God and family most important in your lives. Truly, we share many of the same values and beliefs; only God could have made such a connection.

Having said all that, let us conclude by saying thank you for coming and talking about your future dreams with our daughter. It is at this point that we would like to ask you some questions before we round the next bend in the road.

Questions and Commitments

Why have you chosen our daughter as your partner to marry and spend the rest of your life with?

What do you expect being married to Rachel is going to be like?

Have you considered where you will live after you get married?

What have you learned from your dad and mom about being a husband and a father?

What do you consider your role as a husband and parent should be?

What are your goals for the near and distant future?

Can you assure us that you are going to take care of our daughter financially? Will you work hard, provide for her and your family, and never use money as a weapon?

She doesn't have to live in a castle, but she should have a safe and comfortable home, clothing, and food.

Can you see yourself being happy and content with our daughter, even if life deals you a blow and you both end up being poor?

Will you take care of her emotionally? Two things will destroy your marriage: self-centeredness and bitterness. Guard against these. Inside our daughter's heart is a round hole we call "emotional need." Inside of your heart as a man is a square peg that is somehow going to have to "fit" with her. Are you willing to knock off the edges of that square peg to fulfill her emotional requirements?

She doesn't think or react like you do. You may see something and laugh – she may see it and cry. You may say something that you thought was the sweetest thing in the world, but it may make her very upset. God designed you to be the one who can meet her needs; are you willing to go out of your way to guard against self-centeredness and bitterness and take care of Rachel's emotional needs?

Will you take care of her physically? As a father, it has been my job to protect my "princess." As her husband, your job is to protect your "queen." If someone threatened her, will you step in front of her? By protecting her physically, I also mean intimately. Consider that she is the weaker vessel, as described in the Bible.

> *Likewise, ye husbands, dwell with them according*
> *to knowledge, giving honour unto the wife, as unto*
> *the weaker vessel, and as being heirs together of*
> *the grace of life; that your prayers be not hindered.*
> (1 Peter 3:7)

Will you take care of her spiritually? Do you know that in the Bible, it tells men thirty-three times to love their wives? But it tells wives only twice to love their husbands. You are asking for our daughter's hand. I know what a woman of God she is right now. When I place her hand in yours in marriage, I am no longer responsible for her spiritual health and training. One day, after living together for many, many years, you are going to present her hand to God. Will she be more of a godly woman at that point than the day we gave her to you?

Esther and I strongly believe that you must be the spiritual leader of your family and future children (our grandchildren) according to God's design. Will you take responsibility to read the Scriptures to Rachel and your children? Pray over them? Take them to church on a regular basis?

Will you put forth your best efforts to pray regularly for the salvation and marriage partners of your children?

If you can take care of our daughter financially, mentally, emotionally, physically, and spiritually – as outlined in this letter – then you have our blessing. If you can't, we need to know now.

Appendix D

Brief Outline of the Conference

Session 1: Anabaptism, Culture, and Values

A beautiful culture and family values result from many years of persecution and suffering.

Session 2: Beliefs, Legalism, and Leaving

The gospel according to most Amish has six major elements. Rejecting one could keep a person out of heaven.

Session 3: Evangelism, Stumbling Blocks, and Dos and Don'ts

Why evangelism is necessary and three ways to connect with your Amish community.

Session 4: MAP Ministry and Helping the Former Amish

The start and history of a ministry and how God is moving among the Plain culture.

Dates for upcoming conferences can be found at www.amishawareness.com.

Appendix E

Bible Verses for Further Study and Discussion

Assurance of Salvation

Verily, verily, I say unto you, He that heareth my word, and believeth on him that sent me, hath everlasting life, and shall not come into condemnation; but is passed from death unto life. (John 5:24)

My sheep hear my voice, and I know them, and they follow me: And I give unto them eternal life; and they shall never perish, neither shall any man pluck them out of my hand. My Father, which gave them me, is greater than all; and no man is able to pluck them out of my Father's hand. I and my Father are one. (John 10:27-30)

See also:

Colossians 1:13-14; 2 Corinthians 1:22; Ephesians 1:13-14; Ephesians 4:30; Colossians 3:3-4; 1 Peter 1:4-5, 23; Philippians 1:6; 1 John 3:2; Hebrews 10:14; 2 Timothy 4:18; Romans 10:9, 13; John 3:16; 1 John 5:11-13; Ephesians 2:8-9; Romans 8:1, 16; John 6:37; Acts 2:21; 1 John 2:3-4

Grace

> *Therefore by the deeds of the law there shall no*
> *flesh be justified in his sight: for by the law is the*
> *knowledge of sin. But now the righteousness of God*
> *without the law is manifested, being witnessed by*
> *the law and the prophets; Even the righteousness of*
> *God which is by faith of Jesus Christ unto all and*
> *upon all them that believe: for there is no difference:*
> *For all have sinned, and come short of the glory of*
> *God; Being justified freely by his grace through the*
> *redemption that is in Christ Jesus.* (Romans 3:20-24)

See also:

Ephesians 2:5-9; Romans 5:8; Romans 6:14; Romans 11:6; 1 Corinthians 15:10; 2 Corinthians 12:9; James 4:6; Hebrews 4:16; John 1:16; 2 Timothy 2:1; 2 Timothy 4:22

Faith

> *I am crucified with Christ: nevertheless I live; yet*
> *not I, but Christ liveth in me: and the life which I*
> *now live in the flesh I live by the faith of the Son*
> *of God, who loved me, and gave himself for me.*
> (Galatians 2:20)

See also:

Hebrews 11; Romans 10:17; 1 Thessalonians 1:2-3; Hebrews 12:2

Little Faith

> *And Jesus said unto them, Because of your unbelief:*
> *for verily I say unto you, If ye have faith as a grain of*
> *mustard seed, ye shall say unto this mountain, Remove*
> *hence to yonder place; and it shall remove; and nothing*
> *shall be impossible unto you.* (Matthew 17:20)

See also:

Matthew 8:26; Matthew 14:29-31; Luke 12:27-28

Much Faith

And being not weak in faith, he [Abraham] considered not his own body now dead, when he was about an hundred years old, neither yet the deadness of Sarah's womb: He staggered not at the promise of God through unbelief; but was strong in faith, giving glory to God. (Romans 4:19-20)

See also:

Acts 6:5; Acts 11:22-24; 1 Corinthians 13:2; 2 Corinthians 5:6-7; Ephesians 6:16

Healing Faith

But Jesus turned him about, and when he saw her, he said, Daughter, be of good comfort; thy faith hath made thee whole. And the woman was made whole from that hour. (Matthew 9:22)

See also:

Matthew 9:28-29; Mark 10:52; Acts 14:9-10

Saving Faith

Knowing that a man is not justified by the works of the law, but by the faith of Jesus Christ, even we have believed in Jesus Christ, that we might be justified by the faith of Christ, and not by the works of the law: for by the works of the law shall no flesh be justified. (Galatians 2:16)

See also:

Acts 15:8-9; Acts 20:18-21; Romans 1:16-17; 2 Corinthians 4:13-14; Ephesians 2:8-9

Love
God's Love for Us

> In this was manifested the love of God toward us,
> because that God sent his only begotten Son into
> the world, that we might live through him. Herein
> is love, not that we loved God, but that he loved us,
> and sent his Son to be the propitiation for our sins.
> Beloved, if God so loved us, we ought also to love
> one another. (1 John 4:9-11)

See also:

John 3:16; Romans 5:8; Galatians 2:20; Ephesians 5:2

Our Love for God

> We love him, because he first loved us. If a man say,
> I love God, and hateth his brother, he is a liar: for he
> that loveth not his brother whom he hath seen, how can
> he love God whom he hath not seen? (1 John 4:19-20)

See also:

John 14:15; 1 John 2:15; 1 John 4:16; 1 John 3:10; Matthew 6:24;
Matthew 22:37-39

Love for One Another

> For all the law is fulfilled in one word, even in this;
> Thou shalt love thy neighbor as thyself. (Galatians 5:14)

See also:

1 Corinthians 13:4-13; John 13:34; John 15:12-13; 1 John 4:7-11;
James 2:8; Philippians 2:1-5

Fear

> Fear thou not; for I am with thee: be not dismayed;
> for I am thy God: I will strengthen thee; yea, I will

help thee; yea, I will uphold thee with the right hand of my righteousness. (Isaiah 41:10)

See also:

2 Timothy 1:7; Joshua 1:9; Isaiah 43:1-3; 1 John 4:18; Romans 8:9-15; Philippians 4:6-7; Psalm 23:4; Matthew 6:34; Luke 12:22-26; Deuteronomy 31:6

Appendix F

Free Correspondence Bible Study Courses

Simply check the box by the course you want, fill out the other side of this form, and mail it back to us. We will then send you the first lesson in the course that you requested. Choose one of our current courses:

- ☐ **Bible Basics:** What does the Bible say about forgiveness of sins and being born again? (1 lesson)

- ☐ **ABCs of Christian Growth:** Assurance, Bible, church, daily walk, enemy, family, God, Holy Spirit, all the way to witnessing, and Zion! (24 short lessons)

- ☐ **Life's Struggles:** Find biblical wisdom for overcoming fear, pride, doubt, anger, and worry. (3 lessons)

- ☐ **Book of Books:** Consider the history, customs, geography, and measurements of biblical times. See how the Old and New Testaments fit together. Learn how God's Word applies to your life today. (13 lessons)

- ☐ **Foundational Study:** Study what the Bible says about foundational topics like the new birth, forgiveness, friends, prayer, everlasting life, brokenness, wisdom, lying, salvation, judgment, the

Cut here

Christian home, victory, and getting your life back on track. (3 lessons)

☐ **Verse-by-Verse Study:** Travel verse by verse through parts or all of the biblical books of John, Ephesians, Colossians, 1 John, Titus, and Luke. (9 lessons)

☐ **Topical Study:** Study what the Bible says about topics like how to pray, the Bible is the Word of God, faith, fighting loneliness, doubt and disbelief, fighting temptation, hatred, and more. (12 lessons)

Name _____

Mailing Address _____

City _____ St. _____ Zip _____

Date of Birth _____

Make sure you checked the box by the course you want.

Mail this page to:
Plowman's Academy
PO Box 128
Savannah, OH 44874

About the Author

Joe Keim was born and raised in Ashland, Ohio. He married Esther Keim in 1986 and they left the Old Order Amish community in 1987. They have two grown children, Jonathan and Rachel. In 2001, Joe left his job as a tool and die maker for full-time ministry. The Keims travel all over the US, speaking in churches, as well as to hospital staff, to law enforcement, and at colleges, helping people understand how to communicate with the Amish.

Through personal witness, home Bible studies, home prayer meetings, the Bible Club, *The Amish Voice*, and the Audio Ministry, the Keims want to see every Amish person hear the clear message of salvation. MAP offers counseling and protection to those who are victims of sexual, mental, and physical abuse. The ministry also provides help with needs such as getting a GED, obtaining a birth certificate, and finding a job. Through the Bible Club alone, they have seen more than 2,500 Amish make commitments for Christ.

Photos

All fourteen of us children were born and raised in this two-story house, which still stands to this day. For years, my grandparents also lived in one part of the house.

Our barn.

An aerial view of our home place. If you look close enough, you can see the pond where we trapped muskrats and swam many nights after all the chores were done. This is not, however, the pond where Leander drowned.

This is the shop where I got all my machining and welding experience. In later years, after I left the Amish, my training led me into tool and die making, where I learned to build progressive dies. My company sent me to Chicago for training on EDM Wire and Sinker machines. I also learned how to run CNC equipment and draw up prints with AutoCAD.

Our kitchen and dining area. It was in this area where all our family gathered around the table three times a day for meals. Notice the dark curtains, which were mandatory.

This photo shows my horse, Mike, pulling the two-wheeled cart I built. Crist Byler and I went to school together. He left the Amish at 18 and joined the military. When Crist got out of the military, he stayed in the state of Washington.

This photo was taken when I was 18. The car, a Monte Carlo, was my first. It was during the most difficult and darkest time of my life.

Joe at 18.

This is where my wife, Esther, grew up. It is also the place where we lived for nine months before leaving the Amish for the last time.

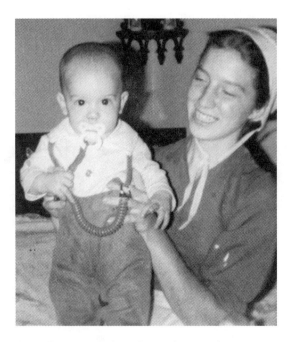

These photos were taken when Esther was about 18 years of age (before our wedding day).

These pictures were taken about three months after our wedding day in 1986.

Up until the day we drove into their driveway with a horse trailer full of our belongings, we had never met nor heard the names Jerry and Carol Gess. We were complete strangers to each other. But from day one, they have made us part of their family.

This picture includes the four Keim brothers who are no longer Amish. Joe and Esther, William and Jenica, Johnny and Miriam, Perry and Maryann, Jonathan and Havilah, David and Rachel, our granddaughter Lily, and nieces and nephews.

This picture was taken the day Rachel vowed to remain sexually pure until her wedding day.

This picture was taken of Samuel Girod the day after he left the Amish and moved into our home. He owned two properties and was in a partnership business with his dad. When he left the Amish, all he had with him were the two duffle bags in his hands.

This photo was taken the day we parked our cars a mile away from the family reunion, walked to sister Ella's house, dressed in Amish clothes, then walked across the field to join our first Keim family reunion. It shows our family, my brother William and family, Johnny and family, and Perry and family. This took place in July of 2008, twenty years after Esther and I left the Amish for the last time.

Esther and Joe today.